THE
Yellowstone River

THE
Yellowstone River
and its Angling

Frank Amato Publications
Portland, Oregon

Andy Anderson

Other books by Dave Hughes:

Western Hatches (with Rick Hafele)
An Angler's Astoria
American Fly Tying Manual
Western Fly Fishing Guide
Handbook of Hatches
Western Streamside Guide
Reading Trout Water
Tackle and Technique for Taking Trout
Tactics for Trout
Deschutes
Strategies for Stillwater

Dave Hughes

About the Author

Dave Hughes is an essayist and a believer in the power of rivers to restore enthusiasm and the love of life. He spent the spring, summer, and fall—which too quickly became winter—of 1991 exploring and fishing the Yellowstone River from top to bottom. Along the way he got blown around by the wind, chased by clouds of mosquitoes, saddle cramped, leg weary, and almost frozen. But also along the way he saw the source of the river, its strangely peaceful headwaters, that vast and restless lake, those sliced canyons, Paradise Valley, and the forgotten other half of the river. He encountered a distinction of animals, and met trout: lots of trout.

Hughes has been writing about rivers and fishing for fifteen years. His articles have appeared in *Flyfishing, Salmon Trout Steelheader, Fly Fisherman, Fly Rod & Reel, Outdoor Life,* and *Field & Stream.* He was founding president of Oregon Trout in 1983, and was honored with life membership by the Federation of Fly Fishers in 1985. He now lives in Portland, Oregon.

Copyright 1992 • Dave Hughes
Front Cover: Dale Spartas
Book Design: Joyce Herbst • Typesetting: Charlie Clifford
Fly Plate Photos: Jim Schollmeyer • Map: Tony Amato
Front Cover Photo: Sue Wynkoop

Printed in Hong Kong
Frank Amato Publications
P.O. Box 82112 • Portland, Oregon 97282
(503) 653-8108 • FAX: (503) 653-2766
ISBN: SB 1878175-22-X
UPC: 66066-00111
ISBN: HB 1878175-23-8
UPC: 66066-00112

Contents

Dedication

◆

To my brother the Montana doctor:
Eugene F. Hughes, Jr.
Without your help this book wouldn't have happened.

Dave Hughes

Acknowledgements

◆

Many friends helped with this book. Gene and Connie Hughes, who own Evel Knievel's former estate in Butte, Montana, provided a home base in the guest house there. Merritt and Barbara Pride, out of their Lost Fork Ranch Lodge on the Madison River, outfitted the difficult trip to the upper Yellowstone and Two Ocean Pass.

Sylvester and Hazel Nemes furnished a spare bedroom in Bozeman, many meals, humor, and an introduction to the Mother's Day Caddis hatch. Vern and Joan Gallup provided a "home away from home away from home" in Island Park, Idaho. They were the source of much comfort; their cabin became the launching point for many trips.

Paul Schullery, fine essayist, author, and Park historian, provided a bibliography of reading for the book, plus a stack of research papers a foot thick. Dr. Wayne Hamilton, Park Research Geologist, helped untangle the difficult geology of the river. John Bailey, owner of Dan Bailey's Fly Shop, gave lots of advice, and provided the right place to go whenever I needed questions answered, help, or a hot cup of coffee. Bob Auger helped every person who appreciates rivers with his patient and successful restoration of DePuy's Spring Creek.

Masako Tani, writer and photographer from Tokyo, Japan, went along on many of the trips. She added humor, enthusiasm, and a contagious sense of astonishment at Yellowstone's wonders. Dan Linnweber and Todd Wester launched me and what became the Blue Iceberg on that last dangerous but wondrously beautiful float trip.

I've gotten into the habit of doing last drafts at beautiful Redside's Retreat, overlooking the Deschutes River. Thank you Ted and Norma, Bruce and Bud. Others I'd like to thank in person.

Yellowstone River

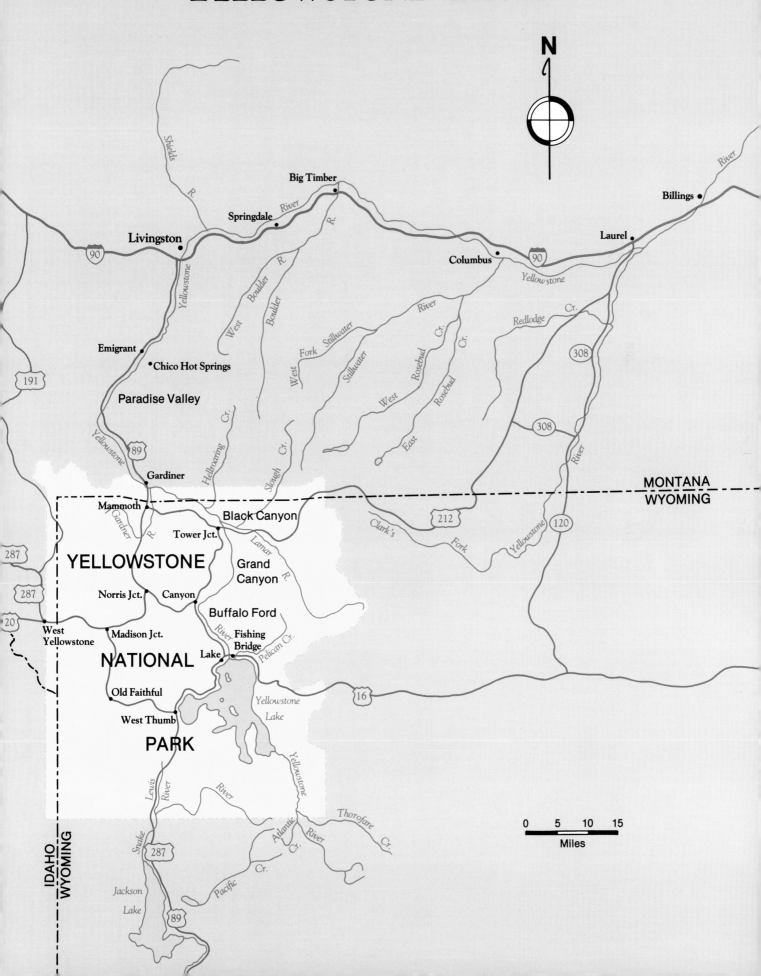

N

Shields R.

Big Timber

Springdale

Billings

Livingston

90

Laurel

Columbus

90

Yellowstone

Boulder River

West Boulder R.

Boulder R.

West Fork Stillwater

Stillwater

Rosebud Cr.

Cr.

Redlodge Cr.

308

Emigrant

Chico Hot Springs

West

West

East Rosebud

Rosebud

308

Paradise Valley

191

Yellowstone

89

Hellroaring Cr.

Slough Cr.

River

MONTANA
WYOMING

Gardiner

287

Mammoth

Black Canyon

212

Clark's

Yellowstone River

120

287

YELLOWSTONE

Tower Jct.

Lamar R.

Fork

20

Norris Jct.

Canyon

Grand Canyon

West
Yellowstone

Buffalo Ford

River

Fishing
Bridge

Madison Jct.

Lake

Pelican Cr.

16

NATIONAL

Old Faithful

Yellowstone
Lake

West Thumb

PARK

Lewis River

River

Yellowstone

0   5   10   15

Miles

Thorofare Cr.

IDAHO
WYOMING

Snake R.

287

Adantic Cr.

River

Jackson
Lake

Pacific Cr.

89

Introduction: **Many Rivers**

When I went to the Yellowstone River to research this book I had already fished it many times over the years. Like most folks, I'd fished the Buffalo Ford area in the Park, drawn some trout to flies in Paradise Valley, seen the edges of Yellowstone Lake, and thought I knew the river. I'd just need to spend a summer seeing some of the missing pieces, and I'd turn the puzzle into a picture.

The missing pieces, I discovered, were the picture: they were the river. Many are seldom seen, never by the casual visitor. To see each part of the river requires a special trip, an extra effort, and time. Some parts take lots of time.

The upper river, for example, meanders through the remnant part of the Park above the lake, far from any road. The source itself lies outside the Park, tucked away even more remotely inside the Bridger-Teton Wilderness of Wyoming. You can get to the upper river by boat up the lake, by horseback, or by a long backpack trip. But you'll never see it if you have to drive to it.

The canyons, both the Grand and Black, are difficult to get

into, more difficult to move along. Violent water butts against cliffs, restricts travel upstream and down. Most access is at points along trails, where you can fish a few pools or runs, then have to climb back up, hike to the next access point, descend to fish again.

The lower river, below Livingston, flirts with the freeway. You can drive to it at many access sites, see a sampling of it from any one of them. But this part of the river is defined by its breadth and patient movement, by the cottonwood islands that divide it into braided channels, by all of the things that separate it from sight when you're driving down the freeway. You've got to Huck Finn it by boat to really see it at all.

When I went to the river I expected to find one that was, like most rivers, defined by a single geography, consistent in character. What I found instead was a succession of rivers, each shaped by a different geography, each with a different character, but all with the same name: *Yellowstone.*

1

*Fire
and
Ice*

*Tortured Ice Age formation of the upper Yellowstone River, with the Ab-
saroka Mountains lining the horizon.* Dave Hughes

*Facing page: A halfmoon stands over the Beartooth Mountains and a low-
water backchannel of the Yellowstone River in fall.* Dave Hughes

Long before either had a name, the Yellowstone River was a small tributary to the larger Lamar, inside what is now Yellowstone Park. The Lamar delivered the waters of both toward a sea to the west, across a land that was flat and alternately scorched by the sun for millions of years, then wet like the tropics for more millions. That was in the era of the dinosaurs, before the Rockies reared up.

The land that is now Montana and Wyoming lay pinned between two seas. The sea in the west, which has since been pushed back to the edge of Oregon and Washington, was the Pacific Ocean, though nobody was around to call it that then. The inland sea to the east, with its edge creeping forward and back near what we call Billings, later receded north toward the Great Lakes and Hudsons Bay, leaving behind the Great Plains.

Events that created the torn geography of the Yellowstone region, out of that narrow flatness of land between two seas, began about

175 million years ago. The continents had gathered into one land mass. Then the Atlantic Rift opened between Europe and the eastern edge of North America. About 90 million years ago the western edge of the North American tectonic plate, galloping away from this rift at perhaps an inch or two per year, collided with the Pacific plate. Continents, though rock, are lighter than the stuff under ocean floors. As a consequence continents float like islands adrift in the dense crust.

The continental plate skidded over the top of the Pacific plate at the site of the collision. The dense ocean plate nosed under, forced down into the hot mantle. It took 20 million years to extract most of the violence out of this accident. The Rocky Mountains wrinkled and arose where the edge of the North American plate got crunched. The diving edge of the Pacific plate melted sixty miles inside the earth, sent great blobs of red-hot rock rising like hot air balloons slowly toward the surface, under the new mountains. These batholiths of molten material caused volcanic activity, some of which has not subsided.

For 10 million years, between 50 and 40 million years ago, the Absaroka volcanic flows extruded rock that would later be uplifted as the Absaroka Range and the northern Beartooths, on the east side of the Yellowstone River, and the Gallatin Range, which forms its western containment. During this period the Yellowstone River was an inland system, flowing into what is now Paradise Valley, and evaporating.

Beginning 10 million years ago, faulting and uplifting shaped the basin-and-range formations that we see today. The Madison River flows north through a broad basin in the morning shadow of the Madison and Gallatin ranges. Paradise Valley is a basin beneath the brow of the Beartooth and Absaroka ranges. This uplift happened recently; it's still happening in places. That's why the mountain country hanging over the Yellowstone River is so torn, so forbidding.

In the last two million years the Yellowstone area has had three catastrophic volcanic eruptions, each 600,000 years after the one before it. The last was 600,000 years ago. We might stand now at ground zero. Later explosions, such as St. Helens in 1981, were pops. They clouded the sun, sprinkled ash. The blasts that formed the successive Yellowstone calderas blocked the sun, laid down layers of volcanic ash for thousands of miles, cooled the climate of the dark continent, perhaps for years.

The current Yellowstone caldera, inside the Park, is about 45 miles long and 20 miles wide. This large vacancy was not created by a mass of land blown away like the lid sent sailing off a pressure cooker. Instead, a great magma chamber melted its way toward the surface, built up terrific pressure and expelled itself through volcanic vents in a ring around the chamber. Hundreds of cubic miles of melted rock exploded into the air through these ring vents. When the eruption ceased, the chamber cooled, and the surface of the earth collapsed into the void, as if the lid dropped into the pressure cooker.

Don't underestimate the shock of these three repetitious events. If another happened tomorrow, ash fallout would smother the farming states. Lack of light and consequent cold would reduce livability in the entire Northern temperate zone. The surviving population of the United States might beg Guatemalans for groceries.

The caldera filled with water and became a vast lake. Succeeding minor events exuded lava into the caldera. Molten material seeped back into the vented chamber beneath the earth and began to lift the surface. Today, parts of Yellowstone Park rise like bread dough at the rate of about an inch a year.

This bull elk grows fat feeding on lush summer grasses in Hayden Valley, in Yellowstone Park. Dave Hughes

Arrowleaf balsamroot blooms along the river in spring and early summer, about the time spring runoff takes it out of shape for fishing. Dave Hughes

Resurgence of the Yellowstone caldera has lifted it from a basin into the Yellowstone Plateau, nearly 8,000 feet in elevation. Resurgence and filling has also reduced Yellowstone Lake, shunting it off to the southeast corner of the original caldera. The lake is still large, but once was much larger. The distinctive West Thumb of Yellowstone Lake is believed to be a separate and more recent caldera inside the larger and older one. It exploded and collapsed approximately 150,000 years ago, within the period of the Ice Ages.

It's a common conception that Ice Age glaciers were sheets of ice that came plodding and plowing down from the north. In part it's true, but those great northern glaciers stopped short of the Yellowstone country.

Glaciers are formed when the average temperature drops a bit and the climate gets wet enough so that more snow falls each winter than melts each summer. This happens in the mountains first. That is where the snow gets deeper, compresses itself into ice and begins to creep downhill. Glaciers that shaped the Yellowstone River formed in the mountains rimming the Park, to the south, beginning around 250,000 years ago. A large glacier crept down the Lamar River. You can recognize its U-shaped valley as glacial today. Smaller glaciers emerged out of all the tributaries to the Yellowstone. A succession of glaciers carved Paradise Valley. They reached a point around Pine Creek, in the valley just north of Livingston, before retreating for the last time.

You can drive up the river and see how this advance and retreat changed your view. Below Pine Creek the valley is flat,

formed by the outwash of water melted from the glaciers. Above Pine Creek the valley is hummocky, its floor formed by masses of material the glaciers transported down from the mountains, then dropped as they melted.

Glacial moraines—hills of material left where a glacier halts its advance and melts—block all of the sidestream canyons coming into Paradise Valley from the east, out of the abrupt mountains. The river downstream from Livingston, on the plains, escaped the pincer of the great glacial sheets from the north and the smaller mountain glaciers from the Park to the south. This lower part of the river shows little sign of the Ice Ages.

The work of glaciers is more apparent in the middle river, Paradise Valley, than it is in the Park. At first glance this seems strange: glaciers started high and traveled to the lower valleys. But the ice in what is now the Park filled the river's canyons and settled in as an ice cap, without much movement, therefore without cutting U-shaped valleys. When the ice cap melted it left deep canyons filled with debris, through which the river eroded new and sharper canyons.

◆

Following page: Sunsets over the Yellowstone can be dramatic because of all the clouds that constantly chase around in the sky. Masako Tani

◆

Buck antelope are a common sight on the flats above the lower river. Ben O. Williams

It seems that the upper river, above Yellowstone Lake, should tumble through the sharpest canyon of all. It does not; the river bottom there is strangely alluvial, like the course of an ancient, lazy river. The reason is simple: the upper river was once lakebed.

Cold bright eye of a golden eagle glares at a photographer malevolently. Ben O. Williams

Yellowstone Lake's outlet was located where Upper and Lower Falls currently tumble into the Grand Canyon of the Yellowstone. Hayden Valley, just above the falls, is flat; it was lakebed. The meandering miles—about 50 of them—upstream from the lake were also once part of the lake. Silt settled onto a flat bottom and leveled it. When the final block broke far downstream, at the falls, the lake dropped and the upper river cut a wandering course across flatness that is more typical of rivers in their final reaches, down in the flatlands.

That is why the Yellowstone River appears oldest where it is youngest, and in some respects youngest where it is oldest.

The oldest records of animal life along the river are in the flatlands of eastern Montana. The river didn't escape its confinement, and burst out into those lands, until the arrival of wetness at the beginning of the Ice Ages, around two-and-a-half million years ago. Still, the beasts that roamed the area provide interest to eras long before the river flowed where it does now.

Before the age of dinosaurs, which began about 250 million years ago, the dominant life forms were called *paramammals*. They marched along an evolutionary path toward mammals. Lizards, or *saurs*, at that time were small and slightly minor beasts. But an extinction hit the earth about 248 million years ago; the paramammals, though not wiped out entirely, lost their dominance and changed our futures.

◆

There's no place more beautiful in fall than the Yellowstone River with its abrupt bluffs and the Beartooths rising up behind them. Dave Hughes

The Lewis Monkeyflower grows brightly alongside small streams at high elevations. You will see it in summer near all of the upper tributaries to the river. Dave Hughes

◆

During the early success of dinosaurs, heavily armored gatorlizards browsed low vegetation. They were hunted by wolflizards nearly twenty feet long. Pterosaurs ran on quick feet toward halting flight. Plants developed elongated stems to outreach the nibblings of dinosaurs, which responded by growing to great size and extending their necks. Tiny and archaic mammals, insect eaters, crouched beneath leaves, watched, and waited their turn to dominate the earth and float the Yellowstone in drift boats.

Toward the end of the dinosaur age, 65 million years ago, massive herds of duckbilled dinosaurs roamed the area between the two seas that confined Montana. They were up to 45 feet long and weighed as much as 25,000 pounds. One group, the *Hadrosaurs*—good mother lizards—apparently took good care of their eggs and young. Another group of small and swift dinosaurs, *Troodons*, slinked around to feed on the eggs and the young. They have been called Cretaceous coyotes.

Dr. Jack Horner, of the Museum of the Rockies in Bozeman, Montana, estimates that a nesting of *Hadrosaurs* might have contained 2,700 adults building more than 1,000 nests in an area less than a mile square. As vegetation got stripped, and the beasts hiked farther for food, *Tyrannosaurus rex* crept near. This fierce lizard, it is speculated, made the nesting site look like a battlefield: huge strewn bodies.

Tyrannosaurus stood on its hind legs, was up to 35 feet long and weighed up to 10,000 pounds. Its head—his and hers— was huge, knife-toothed, stunningly ugly except to each other. Bone structures indicate that, despite its size, *T. rex* could crouch in ambush like a lion. Placid herding dinosaurs succeeded in propagating by gathering so densely that the supply of prey exhausted the appetite of predators. It's the same strategy used by mayflies, which hatch in vast numbers during a compact time frame so that trout simply cannot eat them all.

The age of dinosaurs ended abruptly with an impact explosion 65 million years ago. A slim dark deposit in the world's geological record separates layers below that reveal dinosaur bones from layers above that don't. This thin line contains elements so rare on earth that they could only arrive on a giant meteorite, miles across. The dust cloud spread by the collision turned day to blackest night for weeks and dropped daily temperatures to near zero for a month or two. Dinosaurs might have survived this cold and dark. But plants could not survive the lack of sunlight. Green life died until seeds could push it up again.

Animals that ate plants starved. Predators lost their prey and perished with it. When the dust settled and sunshine returned, it struck a world of plants that survived only as roots and seeds, a world of small animals that lived on those roots and seeds. Birds and small mammals crept forward. Dinosaurs did not.

Mammals burst into this new Yellowstone landscape free of reptilian predation. Predecessors to our bison and elk and deer were hunted by dire wolves and saber-toothed cats. A trapper after beaver could hardly have carried the trap needed to seize the beaver that lived there then. Herds of horses evolved on these plains, migrated across the land-bridge into Asia, into Europe, into Africa where they became zebras. But they became extinct here. Herds of mammoths dominated the Ice Age landscape like fleets of great dark galleons.

Then man walked on.

◆

This dignified picket pin, or ground squirrel, has found a way to make its living by panhandling for groceries in the parking lot at Tower Falls. Masako Tani

2

Man to the Last Moment

This beautiful meadow alongside the upper river was not always friendly to early man: it was and is covered with snow more than half of most years. Dave Hughes

---

Facing page: The Yellowstone River in its canyon reaches was once a migratory path off the plateau for elk, buffalo, and Indians. Dave Hughes

Man entered America during the last glacial advance, when so much water got tied up in ice that the ocean receded. A land bridge opened across the Bering Straight. This wasn't the first time Asia and America got connected, but it was the first time man was around to cross the bridge, probably as several successive bands. They must have stood astounded at the bounty. The startling masses of their favorite food forms—large game animals—tugged them all the way to Tierra del Fuego. But man might have spoiled his own Eden.

It is speculated that the first wandering bands arrived on the continent between 20,000 and 12,000 years ago. They were already experienced big game hunters; that was their income. The animals of Africa had evolved with them and knew to fear them. The animals of Europe, then of Asia, met men and learned to avoid them. But the animals of North America, of the Yellowstone country—mammoths and prehistoric bison, modern elk and deer—had never seen such a sight as these puny beings that gabbled along in talkative flocks. They were not startled. They were probably as tame and fearless as animals in the Park today.

This bull elk in the rut, has just visited a mud wallow to make him more handsome. After the rut he will be somewhat wasted, and his journey out of the park to his wintering grounds will be difficult. Dave Hughes

◆

Men were sudden superpredators. They roamed and hunted in bands, followed the herds, used short spears propelled by *atlatls*: throwing sticks that extended arms and made them more powerful. They hunted in concert, using their brains fiercely as weapons. To seize a single animal, a band often killed a whole herd, for example by igniting a line of fire and driving bison over a cliff.

Around 10,000 years ago, shortly after the entrance of man on this ripe scene, North America suddenly lost seventy percent of its animal species that averaged over one hundred pounds. This abrupt extinction included three species of mammoths, the mastodon, varieties of antelope, shrub oxen, giant peccary,

◆

Perplexed badger aims its burrowing and therefore muddy snout at the photographer waiting patiently for its emergence outside its burrow. Masako Tani

ground sloths, camels, and the beginnings of horses. The climate slowly dried at the same time. But only the favored prey of man, large game species, died out. Plants, small animal species, aquatics, marine species: they lived happily through the demise, with no changes of the kind climate would cause.

Many people who believe in the original innocence of man hope that the slow change in climate caused all sorts of large species to fall over dead at the same time. It's a wonderful thing to wish for, but it's doubtful.

Most large species that survived had some sort of sanctuary from man. A few musk oxen got locked away in patches of open tundra in the far north, behind the ice cap, where man did not migrate until the ice melted, centuries later. Mountain goats and sheep retreated above timberline; they still live in Montana. Deer and elk held out in woodlands, where it's impossible to rout out the last animal. Our present antelope: who could catch them? The buffalo: who can explain their survival? They are the one great bit of logic for the argument that climate did it.

The North American species list of big animals is only an echo of what once roamed the plains. It's too bad a handful of woolly mammoths did not get stashed away behind the ice with the musk oxen, out of harm's way. What grand arguments we could have about what to do with them now.

◆

Lupine grows in clumps in places along the river, turning the banks bright blue. Dave Hughes

Herds of buffalo feed placidly in the Park now, just as they must have when man first stepped onto the Yellowstone Plateau, thousands of years ago.
Dave Hughes

With the climate drying and the great game herds diminished or gone, the plains of the lower Yellowstone River region became inhospitable. Hunting bands moved toward the mountains. Camps 10,000 years old have been found on the slopes around Yellowstone Park, above 9,000 feet. Evidence suggests that the Park has been home to man continuously from that time. Early man was not frightened by those hot steams, geysers, and fumaroles.

These later hunters wintered on the Yellowstone River flats between the Gardner River and Yankee Jim Canyon. They built hunting blinds at springs and in natural passes. They summered in scattered family groups on the Yellowstone Plateau and in the surrounding mountains. They became hunter-gatherers, living on a variety of berries, bird eggs, plants and roots, small game, and big game when they could get it.

They had already tamed the dog, used it to help in the hunt, tote small loads, and bark at strangers. Their shelters and clothes were hides. Their sanitation probably consisted of moving when things piled up. Watch them getting ready to go: women packing things; men striking out light but armed, arguing about the best way to the new place; children eager for the change, laughing, playing, throwing things for leaping dogs, wishing everybody else would hurry.

We don't think of Indians as farmers, except in the southwest. But the first Indian groups to move onto the plains, after the Paleo-Indian hunters had moved to the mountains, followed the soil.

Prairie sod was not soil. It was too thick, too protected by grass roots, to bust without the help of beasts: oxen and horses. So the earliest modern Indians drifted toward the Yellowstone country out of the eastern woodlands, finding soft soil in the river valleys. They planted hardy northern flint corn on the Mississippi beginning about 400 A.D. One group of Hidatsa Sioux migrated up the Missouri and settled in earth-lodge villages in the present Dakotas.

They probably enjoyed about 1,000 years of relative peace. When we got here we called them *savages*. But they would have been astonished to see the slavery, subjugation, and religious persecution driving whites out of Europe in those years. Later, it spilled onto them.

Some of these farmers preferred hunting. About the time white men began stepping onto the eastern shore, small bands of Hidatsa Sioux started spending their winters on the plains of the Dakotas, in pursuit of buffalo and other game. The Crow tribe, which came to live on the lower Yellowstone, has its roots in a couple of these small Hidatsa bands.

The first band, Awatixa hunters, split off and migrated into the lands on the Yellowstone River and up its southern tributaries, into the Wyoming mountains. These became the Mountain Crow. The second group left later and kept the farming tradition longer, settling on the Yellowstone River and in the lands to the north of it. They became the River Crow. The migration and formation of this new tribe took two to three hundred years. It was still shaping itself, adapting to the new land, when two things overtook it.

The horse galloped into the region around 1700. Navajo Indians rebelled against their Spanish masters in 1680, captured their horse herds, and traded them north to the Shoshone. Twenty years later the Shoshone had surplus, traded them to tribes

Preceding page: Six miles of the meandering river in Hayden Valley has been declared off-limits forever to fishing and travel: left as sanctuary to game and fish. Masako Tani

The trail to Cascade Lake is easy. When fishing the backpacking lakes that sprinkle Yellowstone Park, it's helpful to carry a float tube, so you can get out from shore, catch a few more fish and get into a few more adventures than you'd get into if you kept to the bank. Masako Tani

Cascade Lake, a 50-acre body of water that feeds a tributary that enters the Yellowstone in the Canyon Village area, is one of the few waters in the lower US that holds grayling. They are small, but worth the 2-mile hike it takes to catch a few and admire their wildness and beauty. Dave Hughes

around them, including the Crow on the Yellowstone and Bighorn. So the horse, which is part of our bright picture of all plains Indians, came to them just in the instant before white man arrived.

The horse stirred up a stew that had barely settled, perhaps not settled at all. The Crow had just migrated into the Yellowstone region. Their borders bled into the territories of other tribes all around them: the Blackfeet to the northwest, the Shoshone—Snakes—to the west and in what is now the Park, the Sioux to the south, and the Hidatsa to the east. All were hunters but also gatherers. They traveled on foot, thus were not so mobile that they contested their boundaries all that often.

Horses changed that. All of a sudden the tribes were mobile, and all of them turned to buffalo for food. Those great dumb beasts were easy prey to mounted men. With mobility to reach the borders and to cross them, these ill-defined lines suddenly became very important. Tribes that had once been distant relatives, trading partners, and little threat to each other became enemies at the gates, bent on raids, plundering, stealing women, stealing horses. The arrival of horses set tribes in motion and boundaries swirling. And that's the way it's best to view the Indian nations when white men arrived: as a great seething, in violent adjustment.

Whites overtook the plains Indians just after the horse hit them. This was worse. It pinched from several directions.

In order to obtain the wonderful things the white traders offered—rifles, knives, whiskey—the tribes depleted the resources of their own territories, mainly beaver. Then they went poaching into other territories. The seething increased, and became more fatal. Where a coup might have been counted by a touch at an earlier time, it was now more likely to be counted by a scalp.

As white men pondered on, and settled in, the Indian tribes became squeezed. Whites broke the sod and forced Sioux from the south up into Crow territory. The Blackfeet seem to have been knocked loose from all their moorings, partly because Shoshones got horses first and drove Blackfeet off their traditional Montana and Alberta territories. They fought and got them back, but kept on fighting. If the reports of trappers' journals and early

Debbie and Charlie Waterman fish the beautiful restored waters of DePuy's Spring Creek, which was once a dry creek bed, but now offers not only great fishing, but also lots of spawning potential for trout coming up out of the main Yellowstone. Ben O. Williams

histories read right, it sounds like small Blackfeet bands left their women and horses behind, sifted through all the territories on foot, set up ambushes against everybody, fled with light losses, a little loot, and a few scalps.

The worst thing the white man brought was disease. The Crow avoided battle with the whites and in fact turned to the Army and the government to defend their homeland at almost every turn: against the Sioux, against the Blackfeet, against white miners and later white settlers on sanctified territory. Crow scouts led Custer to his battle on the Little Bighorn. Still, the Crow were nearly wiped out. A succession of smallpox epidemics began with the first contact by French traders. By the time Lewis and Clark explored the region in 1806, two to three decades of disease had reduced the Crow from about 16,000 to fewer than 3,000. Our nation, in a way, had only to deal with the remnants of their nation.

The treaty of 1851 granted these remaining Crow all of the lands from the Powder River in the east to the headwaters of the Yellowstone, from the Missouri River in the north to the Wind River Mountains in Wyoming. This treaty was almost instantly broken. Another treaty, in 1868, took away thirty million acres and restricted the tribe to the Bighorn River valley in south Montana.

The Sheepeater Indians were treated just as badly. They were Shoshone who summered high on the Yellowstone Plateau, hunting the mountains. They arrived late, perhaps 1800. They roamed the territory that is the upper Yellowstone, in and around what is now the Park. They had few horses, few rifles. Each band kept fleets of dogs to serve as pack animals. Their contacts with other Indians, especially the marauding Blackfeet, were drastic. Whites harassed them. They became shy and retired to their mountains.

Denigrated as timid, deceitful, dirty, the Sheepeaters were simply folks who retreated into their own way of life, in balance with their own land. As they got pushed farther and farther into the harsher parts of their territory, their lives got more difficult. They were struck often, yet they rarely struck back. They finally surrendered from their sanctuaries in 1879, and left for the reservations of other tribes. No land had been allotted to them.

Sheep have a soft connotation. But these Indians hunted mountain sheep, not domestic sheep. They prowled the high mountain basins with bow and arrow, not rifles. They had the view from up there. Their lives must have been bold, and very free. They raised their children, and moved from camp to camp, in what we now revere as the most beautiful country in the world. Can you hear them getting ready to move?

"Hurry up and pack, Mom; we're moving to a new view."

3

Mountain Men

Modern mountain men must do it the same way they've always done it in the pristine park: spend lots of their time in dances with mules. Dave Hughes

◆

Facing page: Mountain men followed the river up into its smallest bemeadowed tributaries, watching for Indians and searching for signs of fur. Dave Hughes

On his return journey from the Pacific Ocean in 1806, Captain William Clark separated from Captain Meriwether Lewis on the Bitterroot River and explored toward the Yellowstone River. He and his party of a baker's dozen, including Sacagawea, the Sheepeater Shoshone translator, crossed Clark's Fork of the Columbia in the area of Missoula, rode overland to the Beaverhead River and followed it down to the Jefferson River. There Clark resurrected dugout canoes buried on the westward leg and paddled downstream to Three Forks, where the Jefferson, Madison, and Gallatin rivers meet to make the Missouri.

Joined at Three Forks by the men with the horses, Clark's party followed Sacagawea's directions up the Gallatin River, passed over a plain where we put Bozeman later, and gazed down from Bozeman Pass. Then they descended to the Yellowstone River near Livingston. This was July fifteenth, mosquito season.

"I saw two black bear on the side of the

mountains this morning," Clark wrote the day he discovered the Yellowstone River. "Several gangs of elk, from 100 to 200 in a gang, on the river. Great numbers of antelopes." The Crow called it Elk River. *Roche Jaune,* French for yellow stone, is a translation from Minnetaree, a tribe that lived on the Missouri and knew the Yellowstone for the color of the bluffs above the lower river. Lewis and Clark met these Minnetaree on the way up, in 1805. Had they met Crow Indians first, we would call it Elk River.

Clark's party rode downriver from present Livingston four days, then camped. "I determined to have two canoes made out of the largest of those (cottonwood) trees and lash them together. . .canoes of 28 feet in length and about 16 or 18 inches deep and from 16 to 24 inches wide." Take out a ruler, measure the width of your hips, see how much room you'd have to spare in one of those canoes. They were 28 foot lances awash with men, meat, guns, gear. It was wise that he made two and tied them together.

It took only three days to hack these canoes out of trees. Building them proved to be a brilliant idea. "This morning I was informed that half of our horses were absent," Clark wrote the next day. Indians ran them off; Clark suspected Shoshone. The rest of the journey to St. Louis was to be by water.

Clark sent Sergeant Pryor overland with three men and the remaining half of the horses. The canoes and the overland party soon met at the mouth of the Bighorn River. Pryor told Clark, ". . .in passing every gang of buffalo. . .the horses. . .immediately pursue them and run around them. This disposition of the horses is no doubt owing to their being frequently exercised in chasing different animals by their former owners, the Indians. . ."

The area was enriched with buffalo in 1806. Below what is now Billings, Clark's party had to pull their boats onto an island and wait for a herd to cross the river. This herd flowed for an hour, and, "Two gangs of buffalo crossed a little below us, as numerous as the first." Carcasses of buffalo drowned in the crossing floated for days downriver.

Clark spotted a bighorn sheep on a bluff above the river. "I ascended the hill with a view to kill the ram. The mosquitoes were so numerous that I could not keep them off my gun long enough to take sight, and by that means missed." It must have been a mosquito hell.

◆

Bighorn sheep were once prime game for the Sheepeater Shoshone Indians who lived in the rugged mountains surrounding Yellowstone Park. Ben O. Williams

Clark's party floated to the Yellowstone's junction with the Missouri, near what is now the Montana-North Dakota border. They floated down the larger river a ways and set up a camp to await the arrival of Lewis, who was on the Missouri with the main party of men. Sergeant Pryor, left at the Bighorn to ride overland with the horses, arrived first but by boat, and was not afloat by choice. Clark wrote, "At 8 A.M., Sergeant N. Pryor, Shannon, Hall, and Windsor came down the river in two canoes made of buffalo skins. . .Indians had caught and driven off all the horses . . .they killed a buffalo bull and made canoes in the form and shape of the Mandans and Arikaras. . ." Bull boats: the original drift boats of the Great Plains.

Edible morel mushroom. You should never assume a mushroom is not poisoness unless you've identified it carefully with one of the guides to edible species. Ben O. Williams

◆

We've all heard the Yellowstone country described as *Colter's Hell.* It's a mistake. John Colter was an admirable member of the Lewis and Clark Expedition, discharged honorably on the Missouri. While the two leaders dropped down to St. Louis to report their discoveries, Colter went back into the mountains to make more. He spent a winter trapping along the middle Yellowstone.

In October of 1807 trader Manuel Lisa built Fort Raymond at the mouth of the Bighorn River. He hired Colter to track down the various Indian tribes and announce that his trading post was open for business. Colter took off with a thirty pound pack, a rifle, and some ammunition. He trekked 500 miles and became the first recorded white man to travel in the area that is now Yellowstone Park.

Colter's route took him south up Pryor Creek and over to the Shoshone River near Cody, Wyoming. He then turned west up the Wind River, over Union Pass, and down into Jackson Hole. He hiked north up the headwaters of the Snake River, circled the west shore of Yellowstone Lake, and followed the river to an Indian crossing near present Tower Falls. He left the main river, went east up the Lamar River and its tributary Soda Butte Creek, crossed over the Absaroka Mountains to the headwaters of Clarks Fork of the Yellowstone, and dropped back down that tributary to regain the main river, on the plains.

Colter didn't keep a journal, but he described some of the thermal features, thereby proving he had seen them. But nobody believed these stories of steams; it took a long time to prove that *they* were there. What came to be called Colter's Hell was not in Yellowstone Park, but just some puffs on the Shoshone River in Wyoming.

The romantic era of the mountain man was brief, almost abrupt. French Canadians had established trade as early as 1763. They bartered with Indians for furs that got sent out, but left behind diseases that whittled the tribes down to remnants. Lewis and Clark's reports in 1806 opened the area up, but slowly.

Americans crept in and began trapping rather than trading for furs. But they had to creep back out every year to sell them. It wasn't until 1824, the year supplies were first carried overland to a rendezvous where the furs were collected, that the system of fixed posts gave way and mountain men were free to trap and roam most of the year. This was much more efficient. Aubrey Haines, in *The Yellowstone Story*, writes, "It was a system that insured a rapid and thorough ransacking of every nook and corner of the Rocky Mountain wilderness—the Yellowstone Plateau included."

The true mountain man era began with that first rendezvous, in 1824. It ended in 1839 when the first sternwheeler delivered a shipment of supplies to Fort Union at the junction of the Yellowstone and Missouri Rivers, making the overland rendezvous obsolete. By then most of the game was gone. Some mountain men went in ahead of their time; quite a few stayed after their time. I know sorrowful men who still try to live that life today. But the right time for mountain men lasted only fifteen years.

Most mountain men were not the kind to compose careful notes. Traders kept business records. Expedition leaders drew rough maps and wrote diaries. The men out there hunting through the forests, getting their feet frozen in beaver ponds, riding into Blackfeet ambuscades: few wrote it down. But Osborne Russell wrote *Journal of a Trapper*. It's a remarkable record of the life and land: the beauty, the dirt, the danger, the rewards and even the romance; also the ability of the land and its native people to remove those rewards and the lives that pursued them with an arrow or musket ball in an instant.

Russell arrived in the mountains at the height of the era, in 1834. He left in 1843 with the sad note that, ". . .it was time for the White man to leave the mountains as Beaver and game had

A rainbow trout taken in Paradise Valley rests docily in the hand of an angler after making the mistake of taking an artificial fly for the real thing. Scott Ripley

If you're going to hook a fish you want it to be just at the moment a raft happens by, so they'll be astonished and think you do it all the time. Masako Tani

nearly disappeared." His prose is breathless. Reading him is like reading the history of a campaign written by a private rather than the general. You get the view of a single soldier rather than the record of a brigade as if it were a chip slid across the poker table to be bet against another.

Russell, as a newcomer to the mountains, wrote about his first attempt to shoot his own dinner: "I approached a band of Buffaloe. . .shot at a Bull: at the crack of the gun the Buffaloe all ran off excepting the Bull. . .I then reloaded and shot as fast as I could until I had driven 25 bullets at, in and about him which

was all that I had in my bullet pouch whilst the Bull still stood apparently riveted to the spot. . ." No writer could find better words to tell you about the stolid nature of a bull buffalo, or the weak weapons of the era.

Two quotes can inform you about the nature of grizzly bears, and the mountain men who couldn't resist tangling with them. His first encounter: ". . .he was an enormous animal a hideous brute a savage looking beast." Most of us would step around another meeting with that sort of animal.

Drawn to them, the now veteran Russell was later alone, up on a mountain, with a view far down below. He wrote, "I discovered a large Grizzly bear sitting at the mouth of its den I approached within about 180 paces shot and missed it. he looked round and crept slowly into his den I reloaded my rifle went up to the hole and threw down a stone weighing 5 or 6 lbs which soon rattled to the bottom and I heard no more I then rolled a stone weighing 3 or 400 lbs into the den stepped back two or three steps and prepared myself for the out come. The Stone had scarcely reached the bottom when the Bear came rushing out with his mouth wide open and was on the point of making a spring at me when I pulled trigger and Shot him thro. the left shoulder which sent him rolling down the Mountain." That says what you need to know about the nature of those men who went to the mountains.

Russell, with a friend named White, got ambushed by sixty Blackfeet at Pelican Creek, on the north shore of Yellowstone Lake. "At length another arrow striking thro. my right leg above the knee benumbed the flesh. . .the Indian who shot me was within 8 ft and made a Spring towards me with his uplifted battle axe: I made a leap and avoided the blow and kept hopping from

Grizzly! You want to see one of these whenever you're in the Park, yet a great part of you wants not to see one: fears that you'll see one. Ben O. Williams

Drover coaxes the horse team towing a water wagon up the trail that leads to the upper meadows of Slough Creek. Masako Tani

log to log thro. a shower of arrows which flew around us like hail . . .we set down among the logs determined to kill the two foremost when they came up and then die like men. . .About 20 of them passed by us within 15 feet without casting a glance towards us. . .''

Russell and White escaped. Later another trapper, ". . .expressed a wish that I would go with him and two others to make a hunt in the Yellow Stone mountains I replied I had seen enough of the Yellow Stone Mountains.''

Jim Bridger was a brigade leader. Russell trapped under his leadership. Later Bridger became a scout, a guide, a hunter, a teller of tall tales. Because many of Yellowstone's most famous and spurious stories got attached to him, Bridger became known as both a hero and a scoundrel. The truth probably lands on one at times, the other when it wants to. It's clear that he outlived the time of the mountain man and went on to become the time's clever spokesman. What he did—leading those brigades—was true. What he told was often not.

He told apocryphal tales to open-eyed tourists. Quoted in *The Yellowstone Story*, Bridger declared, "In many parts of the country putrifactions and fossils are very numerous. . .a large tract of sage is perfectly petrified, with all the leaves and branches in perfect condition. . .while the rabbits, sage hens, and other animals usually found in such localities are still there, perfectly petrified . . .and more wonderful still, these petrified bushes bear the most wonderful fruit—diamonds, rubies, sapphires, emeralds. . .''

The mountain man era dwindled into stories to be told. Many men, Russell among them, went on west to the new territories, or followed the mad leads of the various gold rushes. Others stayed, Bridger among these, to find ways to make a living, to help tame the mountains and the plains.

The end of the Civil War released thousands of men onto the plains. They harnessed horses and oxen, broke the sod. They

pushed the Sioux up into Yellowstone country from the south. Miners and settlers and adventurers set the Blackfeet adrift from the west. The land of the Crow Indians became cramped, ablaze with wars. They refused to fight whites.

The Sioux did not. They finally got cornered in a camp of thousands, in a mixture of tribes under a conclave of chiefs, along the Little Bighorn River. It was 1876. Crow scouts led a bold blonde general to the site, then were dismissed, mission accomplished. The scouts retired. The battle was brief.

Made righteous by defeat, whites drove Indians onto their reservations, kept them there and made the Yellowstone country safe for themselves.

Big cutthroat trout about to detonate on a grasshopper that has made a fatal mistake. It kicked off into the air only to ride the wind into water. Dale Spartas

4

Gateway to Trout

Cutthroat trout move out of Yellowstone Lake and into tributaries to spawn in spring. When finished they stack up in pools like this one on Thorofare Creek just above its junction with the Yellowstone. It's a tough trip in, but it's good fishing once you get there. Dave Hughes

Facing page: Two Ocean Creek where it plunges down out of the hills, just before its division into Atlantic and Pacific Creeks: the gateway to trout into the Yellowstone River. Dave Hughes

Let's grab a plane, go look at the headwaters.''

A few minutes later the wheels of the Cessna 210 thumped into their wells, brother Gene twirled the plane once around the Butte basin for altitude to clear the Rockies, then shot for a gap in the Tobacco Roots that delivered us high over the Madison River. Gene dipped his wing to scout some elk basins in the Madison Range, then arrowed over Hebgen Lake, over West Yellowstone, over Old Faithful and the headwaters of the Firehole River.

At the south boundary of the park Gene picked up the Snake River and followed it twisting eastward to its sources as we would soon follow it on horses. He circled Mariposa Lake, on the Continental Divide, from that altitude an emerald pendant to hang on your neck. An instant later in aerial time we were high over the Yellowstone, where water flowed toward a different ocean. Gene banked south, flew up the meandering river, following its narrowings toward Younts Peak.

We flew over the top of the mountain. Younts Peak rises up gently from one side as an alpine prairie, gold with grass, high above timberline. It falls away abruptly on the other side, which is where the ice basins cling that are the sources of the river. It's all above 12,000 feet.

"There it is!"

"No, that's not it. This is it over here."

We gazed down into basin after pitched basin, at creeklet after rushing creeklet. We searched for the exact source of the Yellowstone River. We soon concluded, as one must always conclude about rivers, that it has many sources. But we agreed that one glint of water winked at us from the highest ice field, on the scarp of Younts, and fell farther than the others before joining them and mingling its pure waters with their pure waters. We could have been right, we could have been wrong.

Gene pointed one wing at the sun, the other at the core of the earth, and swirled while I madly snapped pictures. When my stomach had gone to where my brain had been and my brain had flown out the top of the plane I told Gene, "I've got enough. Let's go find Two Ocean Pass."

My parts had not quite reassembled themselves when we found the junction of Atlantic Creek with the Yellowstone and followed the smaller stream to the Continental Divide. There we saw a swampy meadow that is Two Ocean Pass: the gateway for trout into the Yellowstone River system.

The prehistoric Yellowstone had no trout. Cutthroat are native to the Pacific coast. The Yellowstone is an Atlantic river, on the other side of the Rocky Mountains. Trout, in nature, can't hike or take the train. They've got to swim wherever they go. Cutthroat trout got across the Rockies and into the Yellowstone about eight to ten thousand years ago. They swam up the Columbia, up the Snake. They got to the top. Somehow, they spilled over into the Yellowstone. How?

Dr. Wayne Hamilton, research geologist at Yellowstone Park, expressed to me the chance that trout arrived when ice sheets backed up Yellowstone Lake during the last Ice Age. The lake's overflow might have been sent west. Trout would have entered easily from the Snake River system. Dr. Hamilton reckons it a possibility, not a fact. I looked at his hands while talking quietly with him in his office at Mammoth. They are weathered, strong, scarred hands. You have to give credence to possibilities raised by a man who is out there chipping away at the earth's secrets.

Trout can cross at this moment at Two Ocean Pass. It is romantic to think that they first migrated from the Pacific to the Atlantic watersheds at a place where we can dip a cooling handkerchief into water today, or cast a coaxing fly.

From the air, circling with Gene, too much of the swampy meadow was masked by timber, and willows. We could see Pacific Creek descending toward the Snake River and Jackson Hole. We could see Atlantic Creek dropping toward the Yellowstone. But we could not see where the streams split. We'd have to get closer.

The strangely alluvial headwaters of the Yellowstone River are a result of many centuries spent as the bed of a lake, before an ice block gave way at what is now upper and lower falls. Here Atlantic Creek meanders in to join the Yellowstone. Dave Hughes

Lost Fork Ranch pack string crosses the Snake River on its way to the distant upper Yellowstone River and Two Ocean Pass. Dave Hughes

A flat tire on the eight-horse trailer cost an hour and a delayed departure from the trailhead on a long ride. A couple of backpackers from Europe, not knowing about horses, hiked through the pack string causing a rodeo. Wranglers Steve and Hubert cussed the string back together and we struck off again. Two days later we rode through a beautiful mile of meadow near the headwaters of the Snake River. We set up camp that night in near darkness and took quickly to the tents.

A sharp crack, then a crash, woke me. It was followed by a burst of both laughter and cursing striking together through the night. It was one o'clock. I went back to sleep. In the morning the disaster was obvious: the last of four heavy food boxes, hoisted high onto the bear pole by sleepy wranglers, had cracked it, pitched all the boxes to the ground, shattered dozens of eggs, scrambled our food supply. It was Steve who laughed. "What else could I do?" he said. It made sense to me. But not to Zack, the cook whose kitchen got reduced to rubble.

The next noon Masako, Gene, his oldest son Trevor, and I hiked a couple of miles up to Mariposa Lake, that jewel set in an alpine meadow that we'd seen earlier from the air. The little emerald is shaped like a teardrop, its overflow crying in a steep plunge toward the Snake. Like most high mountain lakes in August, it holds active, almost eager trout.

Gene frisked my fly boxes and absconded with a size 8 Black Woolly Bugger, which he fished on a dry line. It's not a bad way to start on any stillwater. He was the first rigged and casting, and he was the first to begin leading trout toward shore. They were small, eight to ten inches long, perfect as the lake they reluctantly left. Their skins were the deep rich gold of sunlight on wheat; their cheeks blushed; their gill slashes were bright red. Bold black spotting erupted faintly at mid-fish and exploded toward their tails.

Fringed gentian, the official flower of Yellowstone Park, grows in a grass meadow alongside a small tributary stream. Masako Tani

Preceding page: Yellowstone River heads in a basin high on the slopes of 12,000' Younts Peak. . .though in the view from the air there are many similar basins that might give rise to the river. Of course all of them do; only spring creeks have a single source. Dave Hughes

The Yellowstone River above the lake is strangely peaceful for the upper reaches of any river. Masako Tani

I tried a No. 10 Black Gnat wet fly on a wet-tip line, letting it sink, retrieving it at a staccato clip. Every few casts a quick tug told of a take. The trout that came thrashing up, and went dashing back toward the depths when I released them, were the same gems as Gene's, no bigger.

Masako worked her way down the shore toward the grassy point from which I'd been fishing. She cast a generic dark nymph on a dry line, let it settle, drew it slowly back. Do you know that women send out fewer frightening pheromones than men? A fly tied onto the leader by a feminine hand will often take more and larger trout than one tied by a male hand. So I was not surprised when Masako arrived, cast to the water I'd already scoured, and almost instantly hooked a trout that would swat the ones I'd been catching out of its way.

She led that fish flapping toward shore and held it in her hands while I took pictures. It was fifteen inches long, so fat its belly sagged around her fingers, a truly beautiful trout agleam in the sunshine before she released it.

Not long after that, thunderclouds rushed over the nearby divide. Gene, with the weather eye of a pilot, said, "We better get out of here." We did, dropping down the trail almost at a trot, reaching the tents just as a hailstorm struck. The abrupt onset of the storm left the fishing at Mariposa Lake as one of those isolated instants in time: remote, beautiful, and brief.

That night Connie, Gene's wife, rode in with Graham and Diana, the youngest of their children. They'd covered nearly forty miles to catch up in one day what we had ridden in two days. Most of their ride was on horses spurred to a trot, the last two hours in the same hailstorm that drove the rest of us to tents. They were exhausted, drenched, frozen. The next morning they hoisted sore rumps onto the same saddles without complaint, and we all rode on toward the upper Yellowstone.

The Continental Divide itself was not dramatic where we crossed. We had to look twice to know we'd done it. A dry draw rose from the west toward a small patch of trees. We rode through the trees. A small stream trickled east out the other side of them. That was all. No dramatic views tumbled away toward opposite oceans.

When we dropped into the broad valley of the upper Yellowstone, we found it muddied from the same storm that drove us off Mariposa Lake. It wasn't fishable. I didn't have any idea how long it would take to clear. Camp was a couple of miles up Thorofare Creek, above its junction with the Yellowstone. Thorofare heads east up into the mountains of Wyoming. Its flow is placid in the old lake bed, where we camped, but it drains some of the most remote wilderness in the world.

The next morning Gene, Masako, and I rode out early with Hubert, the head wrangler, toward Two Ocean Pass. The trail followed the Yellowstone, meandered up through meadows, through timber burned in the 1988 fires. The sun rose and struck down through the water, right to the bottom. The river had cleared overnight. As we rode along it, occasional dark arrows flew out from the banks and sank into the depths. These were trout fleeing from the thudding of horse hooves on the bank above them.

At Atlantic Creek we turned away from the larger river and rode upstream through timber, alongside water that tumbled eagerly toward the distant ocean. After an hour we broke into the swampy meadow that sits astride the divide, that drops creeks in both directions.

The meadow is a half mile long. It looked like cropped grass from the air, but from the back of a horse it was a dwarf-willow flat, with a half dozen streamcourses hidden under the brush. The trail crossed two of them that were distinct: the headwaters of Atlantic Creek and Pacific Creek. They were just one hundred yards apart. We tethered the horses. Hubert snoozed on the pine needles. Masako, Gene and I followed Pacific Creek up toward the Parting of Waters.

A sign marked it, but we didn't need it. Two Ocean Creek plunged down a steep hillside, four feet wide. It separated into two creeklets, each two feet wide, as if around an island. But it never got together again.

A cow moose that lacks any bashfulness noses around camp while its confused calf keeps its distance. Masako Tani

Yellow columbine sprinkled beauty along the trail we hiked to Mariposa Lake, high near the Continental Divide where the western drainage of the Snake River crosses over to become the east-flowing Yellowstone. Masako Tani

Masako and I spotted a school of trout darting around in a tiny pool in Atlantic Creek, just below the junction. They were about four inches long. These were trout that had a choice; some would become Snake River fish, others Yellowstone fish. We rigged our rods, stepped out into the meadow, fished Atlantic Creek. Trout came to our flies, but they were the same four inchers we'd seen in the pool: large enough to carry the seeds of a species across the Continental Divide, but not really big enough to pester with flies.

We quit, joined Gene and Hubert, rode down Atlantic Creek toward its junction with the Yellowstone. Back on the flats, among the dwarf willows, we astonished a moose, then rode by a deep bend pool and spotted the quivering surface that indicates restless trout down below. We dismounted eagerly, strung pack rods, tied on flies, began casting. The trout were surprisingly difficult.

We cast Woolly Buggers, dry flies, large wets, but forgot to try nymphs. Gene finally hooked a fish on a small soft-hackle with an olive chenille body and a turn of pheasant rump hackle. Masako hooked another on a Woolly Bugger fished very slowly, her specialty. Gene caught a final fish on his soft-hackle, then a thunderstorm struck, their specialty. The trout were all cutts, all beautiful fish up from Yellowstone Lake for the spawning run. They averaged sixteen inches long, between a pound and two pounds weight.

Hubert led us through the storm back to camp, our mission to see the Parting of Waters accomplished. The rain was heavy, splatting onto our slickers, our saddles and horses. But it was brief.

The next day was a layover day before starting the long ride back. Masako and I awoke to cries from Gene and the kids. They were down at a bend on Thorofare Creek already, and already into fish. The run they cast over was long, deep, butted into a cutbank on the far side. Trout were stacked in it, nervous from the closeness of too many other trout in too small a space, moving, their movements reflected in swirls on the surface, then returning to where they started, their fins aquiver. Flies drawn through them were ignored some of the time, but often enough drew savage strikes: violent surprises.

Most trout in the upper river, and in its tributaries like Thorofare, are not resident. They live in the lake and move up to spawn as soon as the water begins to drop after snowmelt torrents tear through. At this elevation—nearly 8,000 feet—spring comes late. Runoff typically lasts until early July. Trout finish spawning and back down from the tributaries soon after that. They hang out for weeks in the bemeadowed upper river, furnish it with fish out of proportion to its meager carrying capacity.

These lake fish are far larger than you would expect from the size of the stream. They average sixteen inches. The largest weighed over three pounds. Gene took it on a Royal Wulff dry, at the junction of Thorofare Creek and the Yellowstone. At times the trout were anxious to feed, and we caught them on anything. We encountered a few moments when they were dour for some reason. But these times were brief. Most of the time these hungry trout came quickly to flies.

Heed a couple of cautions about the upper river. First, the silty bottom can get stirred up by a storm. It also comes back into shape quickly. If you go there, give yourself a few fishing days so you'll be sure to have some time when the water is clear. Second, mosquitoes are fierce in the marsh that is the old lakebed. We went into the area in late August, after the sun had a chance to bake the meadows dry. Mosquitoes were not a problem. In July, when you can first fish the river, they might carry off your camp.

The best timing for a trip into the upper river has to hit a fairly narrow window: after the runoff ends in July, before the trout back down in September. I would advise the last two weeks of August. You'll see slightly fewer fish, but still catch plenty. You won't get devoured by mosquitoes. In September the weather becomes risky, and the numbers of trout dwindle.

A tiny feeder stream that in time becomes Lynx Creek and then the Yellowstone drains out of the timber where the trail up the Snake River crosses over the Continental Divide into Yellowstone country. The Divide itself is in the notch in the trees at the top of the photo. Dave Hughes

5

Track of the Evening Star

Though Yellowstone Lake is a large one, you can get some of the best fishing right off shore, with tourist vehicles nearly in your backcast area, because the insects and crustaceans that trout eat gather in the shallows along the shoreline. Masako Tani

◆

Facing page: Bull moose feeds in shallow lagoon at the edge of vast Yellowstone Lake. Dave Hughes

Next in line is the lake. The upper river flows into it. I wanted to see the spot where that happens. I wanted to fish there. But it took quite a while to get there. And I didn't fish when I did.

I went to the lake first in early June, when the road to it had opened but the roads beyond it were still buried beneath snow. The lake itself was a vast sheet of ice covered with snow: white, glaring in the sun. A small bay of open water worked its way up from the river, where the water gathered speed and moved too fast to freeze at June night temperatures. The rest was locked in, though by then there likely were openings out beyond sight where hot springs bubbled up from the bottom.

In early July, friends and I went to nibble at the lake's edge. If fishing can be compared to a piece of cake, and catching lots of fish can be compared to eating the frosting, I discovered quickly that the edge of Yellowstone Lake is the best place to bite.

Masako and I ate dinner with Jim and Gay

Snyder in the beautiful Lake Hotel. We got up late the next morning and drove out to the lakeshore just to take a look.

I do lots of my looking through binoculars. I've always got a pair of miniature Nikons dangling around my neck, especially in a place like Yellowstone where the view often opens onto herds of buffalo, browsing bull elk, a moose in a swamp, a coyote mousing a meadow. So I stood next to the road where it rims the lake and aimed my binoculars down at the shallows. Flotillas of small insects tossed on the slightly rippled surface. I focused closer. They were mayflies. Without binoculars I would not have noticed the insects. Without my attention drawn to the insects I would not have noticed the tiny dimples that appeared among them.

Those dimples were the snouts of trout feeding on becalmed mayflies.

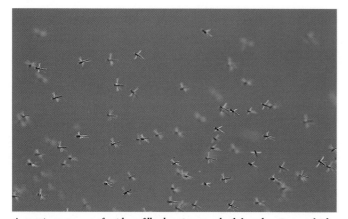

A mating swarm of midges fills the air over the lake; the air can fairly hum with them, with the sound of high-tension wires high overhead. But trout like them, especially in their aquatic pupal stage, just before they leave the water and take to the sky. Ben O. Williams

We scrambled for fishing gear. Gay stood on a rock near shore, cast a size 8 Olive Woolly Bugger far out, retrieved it back at a trot, and got into the first fish. It whacked her fly, goaded a shout out of Gay, came thrashing to her hand. It was a fat fish, pushing a couple of pounds. She continued to cast her Woolly Bugger and continued to interrupt the wanderings of occasional trout the same size. But Jim solved the riddle, causing the fish to be easy.

He stood on a rock near shore, like Gay. Rather than cast out, however, he hovered like a heron, watched the water, held his fly in reserve, ready to cast. Whenever a trout cruised into view Jim dropped a dry fly gently to the water a few feet ahead of it. He let it rest a moment. Then he twitched the fly to attract the attention of the approaching trout. Most of the fish turned toward the fly without hesitation. Most of them took it confidently, poking their noses out to inhale the dry as if it were a natural. Then detonations happened.

Cutts don't jump much, but Jim did.

The fly wasn't critical, but it had to have the approximate size and shape of the mayflies on the water. A size 14 Adams fooled them; a Royal Wulff didn't. They snubbed an Elk Hair Caddis, but smacked their lips over a Blue-Wing Olive. The insects were Speckle-wing Quills *(Callibaetis)*. The best dry dressings were Speckle-wing Compara-duns and Olive Harrop Hairwing Duns, size 14.

The hatch tapered off around two o'clock, but the fishing didn't. Gay continued to surprise a few fish on her Woolly Bugger. But Masako reckoned right when she said, "With all these duns around, the trout must be taking lots of nymphs before they hatch." That's what worked after the hatch: nymphs.

It was easy to fish them. Most of the time we cast them out, let them sink a bit, retrieved them back with twitches of the rod tip. Takes were solid, snapping the rod down. But it was more fun to stand in the shallows, spot a cruising fish, cast the nymph

The shallow pebble-bottomed coves of Yellowstone Lake are enormously productive, rich in insect life, full of cruising and feeding cutthroat trout. Stalking the shallows and casting right to the edge is usually the best way to take trout. Dave Hughes

Sun sets behind a thunderhead collapsing off the edge of the Yellowstone caldera. Thunderstorms can rise almost every afternoon over the lake, during the summer, giving good reason to be watchful whenever you're out on the lake in a small boat. Masako Tani

ahead of it, then retrieve across its bow. We fished Hare's Ear Nymphs this way, and they worked. But we had better luck with size 12 Olive Hare's Ears and some Olive Scud patterns that I suspect the trout mistook for mayfly nymphs ambling along.

The wind rose and flung itself across the lake about four o'clock, piled waves against our shore, ending fishing abruptly.

A week later Masako and I took another nibble at the lake with Vern and Joan Gallup. The sun was bright, the water clear. Speckle-wings hatched again. Trout cruised, but not so close to shore. Vern inserted himself into a float tube, fished the shallows, but farther out. He kept a constant bend in his rod with small Woolly Buggers.

Masako nipped far down the shore, found a pod of fish close to shore and fooled half a dozen with the same dries that had worked a week before.

I didn't enjoy so much success. But one trout made itself memorable by spearing up to take my dry from somewhere in the depths. It was a dark form appearing into a shaft of sunlight and swimming up it as visible as if it climbed inside a glass pipe. It attacked the fly, turned down still visible in the streak of light, then became a streak itself when it felt the hook.

Clouds built suddenly over the lake. The wind struck like a snake. Lightning played around the islands. Vern paddled in. Masako reeled up. We all joined Joan in the car and decided to drive home.

On the way we crossed a causeway out over a shallow curve of lake. Fishermen lined it, tossing bright wobblers, big plugs, dunking unhappy and illegal worms. Vern spotted trout rising right off the causeway, among the waves of the storm. He stopped, the two of us rigged up quickly and jumped off the cement breakwater into shallow water. Our backcasts darted between cars crossing the causeway. We both hooked trout almost instantly, played them to hand, released them. Then we looked at each other with the same idea forming in our heads. "Let's get out of here," Vern said.

A wave of excited chatter and renewed enthusiasm ran along that line of anglers as a wind shiver runs over water. Vern and I were smart enough to leave before a few fruitless casts proved us mortal.

You can see a vast lake by standing on its shore, and fish it well enough. But you can't *know* it until you've been on it. So Masako and I visited the ranger station at Grant Village, planned our camps for a five day trip, then hired a power boat to haul our twelve-foot drift boat to distant Plover Point. We arrived an hour before dark, but were three miles across an open arm from our assigned camp.

Following page: The snowy Absaroka Mountains crouch down nearly to the edge of Yellowstone Lake, and carry snow throughout much of the year. Dave Hughes

An adult osprey and its fledgeling rest in their nest perched on the top of a burnt tree abruptly above the edge of Yellowstone Lake. Dave Hughes

Stuff got piled into the boat in a hurry. In minutes we were off, rowing across the windless water, the boat so laden that furious rowing resulted in plodding progress. But it put us on the far shore just at dark, before any ill wind had a chance to rise and drive us all the way across the lake, which became our constant fear.

We landed on a sand beach, got out to look for our tent site and were greeted by a cloud of mosquitoes. Masako lit a mosquito coil, but it did no good in the open air. I swept moose pellets out of the way and pitched the tent, then built a fire, which drove the pests away, which is something you'd better remember if you're going to make this trip in July: a smoky fire is the most effective mosquito repellant.

We sat in lawn chairs near the fire until the coolness of the mountain night put all bugs to bed.

The next morning we were up at five o'clock to get on the water before the wind. Mosquitoes were up earlier, so we struck the tent and launched in a scramble to get onto the water. We ate breakfast offshore, then rowed around a timbered point that unfolded its curve so slowly we thought we would never get into

the Southeast Arm, the eight-mile reach of water that receives the upper river. We finally arrived at the arm around ten o'clock, but the wind was already there. It punched us in the nose.

I fought it for an hour, got half a mile up the arm. The boat bucked on the waves, but there's nothing safer in a chop than a boat that's designed to take rapids in rivers. Of course, a drift boat is not designed for fighting winds. I rowed past a pretty beach, put my back into the oars for twenty more minutes, but that beach kept right up with me.

I gave up. It was the first morning. We were far from the river's entrance. But I knew there would be no way to row against that wind for eight miles. I'd die.

The wind angled us onto the beach in seconds. Masako cooked a brunch while I studied the map and pondered alternatives. After I'd decided that all we could do was rest where we were for awhile, then turn back, I built a fire in case a mosquito might dare the wind. None did, but as we sat talking half an hour later it suddenly seeped into us that the smoke from the fire blew up the arm. The wind had shifted. We didn't even talk about it. We doused the fire in a cloud of steam, jumped into the boat and chased after that cloud but failed to catch it.

Two hours later, halfway to where we wanted to go, we got

Sometimes a spinner fall of mayflies is so heavy on the lake that your hat and shirt get sprinkled with them, as they rest from their ritual of dancing and mating in the air. Dave Hughes

From the air, it is quite clear where the upper Yellowstone River enters the lake. From the water, the delta looked like a confusing maze. The author rowed right past the river itself, and followed up one of the false leads. Dave Hughes

punched by the wind again. At first we felt suckered. Then we felt discouraged. But we were too close to our goal to give up. So we put the wind against a gunwhale and tacked across the three-mile wide southeast arm. It took two hours. I knew if a storm came up that tub of a drift boat would ride it out. You wouldn't ever want to expose yourself on open water that long in a canoe, except at dawn when the lake is still.

The long tack put us onto a lee shore. It took two more hours to follow its convolutions around to the mouth of the river. But our goal, once reached, proved to be ill defined.

The meeting place of river and lake is a vast delta, more than a mile across, with so many branches and false leads that in the end it misled us on our search for the incoming river. We hiked up onto a hill above this delta, swatted at a deviltry of deer flies and got a broad view. Two moose fed out in the shallows, one a big bull. Geese, ducks, swans and pelicans rested on the grass flats. A channel on the far side was obviously the river. It went up into the willow bends where the river meandered out of the trees.

We dropped down the hill, rowed across the entire front of the delta to this channel, fighting the wind again, only to find it a false lead and the river somewhere behind us. But we had seen no current.

It was nearing night. The Yellowstone River obviously transformed itself into Yellowstone Lake somewhere up one of those mysterious leads. It might take a day to find it; we only had an hour of light left, and we hadn't found our assigned camp for the night yet. We ate dinner on shore, watched a moose wade across the lead we had mistaken for the river, watched a flock of pelicans come in low around a corner, spot us, flare whitely right above us. Then an enchanting thing happened.

The wind died. A spinner fall of tiny mayflies descended out of the trees that rimmed the shoreline darkly. Rises, hundreds of rises, speckled the water in the quiet and the gathering dusk. We launched again and rowed gently after the rising fish.

The trout were selective and not easy. Masako cast while I rowed, dropping her fly down in size until she began getting soft takes to a size 18 Adams. Then the fish were easy. But by then it was too dark to see the fly. She quit fishing. We eased along the shore, watching the water, surprised by rises that continued so near the boat, so eager.

Darkness closed in completely, and we still had not found camp. But in such soft beauty it became all right. The wind was still; the lake was calm; the night was wonderful. The evening star rose over a black point of land behind the boat, in the east, and began its trip across the southern sky. I put it over the stern, struck out into open water, let it guide me back across the wide southeast arm.

All of the trout in Yellowstone Lake are pure-strain Yellowstone cutts, with their bodies spotted black. It's very difficult to catch a legal one: shorter than the maximum length, 13". Masako Tani

◆

You can wade out knee-deep into the vastness of Yellowstone Lake, and spot trout cruising right around your feet. Twitch a fly ahead of them and you're likely to cause a detonation. Masako Tani

A pelican sails along gracefully above the lake, looking for trout, the same as you. Masako Tani

◆

The moon rose, just a thin slice from being full. Masako spread a sleeping pad and bag across the wide stern seat of the boat and went to bed. I held that star over the stern and rowed on for hours. The star rose higher into the sky, southeast toward southwest, and curved my course slowly from westward to northward as it climbed above the stern. It was the perfect trajectory: I picked up the far shore of the arm, a black line of trees in the moonlight, and slowly sliced on a bias toward it, the star still on my stern. At midnight the star reached its apex, and I rowed straight north up the arm, close to shore, the track of the star still guiding me.

At one o'clock, I quit and we camped.

The rest of the trip we fished. One day we got into a Speckle-wing mayfly hatch in the curve of a pebble-bottomed bay. The wind was calm; the sun struck through the water to ignite the bottom. Dark forms cruised above it. Noses poked out to inhale the helpless insects. We stunned dozens of those noses with dry flies cast into cruising lanes.

On another shore we discovered cruisers that swam deep, not feeding on top. We anchored the boat and took turns watching patches where the sunstruck bottom revealed trout as they passed above it. We cast Olive Woolly Buggers until we ran out of my meager supply of them. Then we switched to Polly Rosborough's Green Damsel in size 8, and coaxed fish after fish to the stripped fly. The takes were often visible, though far down in the water.

The last day a violent wind sprang up and forced us to shore on a long strip of sand beach. A backwater lagoon behind the beach seethed with rising trout. Thunderheads built above the lake. Lightning flashed across the southern sky, headed our way. We couldn't risk the lake in such wind, not because the boat wouldn't take the waves, but because we might be blown clear across the lake. So we tied the boat securely to a tree, rolled up our pants, grabbed our rods, and waded barefoot into the lagoon. The trout responded eagerly to our flies, and we played one after another while the sky got darker and the lightning closer.

Suddenly rain burst onto our heads and we rushed out of the lagoon toward the boat, after our slickers. I saw a rise near the shore, cast as I ran, hooked a fish, and played it on the run, releasing it, getting drenched. By the time we got our raingear on and spread a tarp to cover our equipment in the boat, the rain stopped as abruptly as it started. The lightning flashed past and went north. We looked around in surprise at the sudden calm, then went back to the lagoon and educated more trout.

Almost always Masako trolled a streamer or large wet fly while I rowed. She hooked so many trout that I kept rowing while she played them, laughing at her antics as she tried to net them while the boat skidded along, stopping only long enough to make sure they got released back into the water gently, unharmed.

Regulations on Yellowstone Lake allow keeping two trout *under* thirteen inches long. It's rare to catch a keeper. I recall only one because we got so excited about it: it was small enough to keep. Most of the trout we caught were between fifteen and seventeen inches long. But big fish, over three pounds, were also scarce. There are no substantial food forms larger than insects, so cutts don't get to turn into piscivores—fish eaters—and suddenly balloon as they do in some lakes.

Yellowstone Lake doesn't offer great fishing the entire season. It opens June 15, or as soon thereafter as the ice melts. Trout are right on the shorelines, cruising for food, for the next few weeks. Toward early August, as the water warms up, they begin to back down toward the depths. You will always find a few cruising the shallows, but it becomes less common, and the best way to fish is to go out in a tube or boat, drop down a fast sinking line and weighted fly, then troll slowly, letting the fly fish for you. It's not so much fun.

It's time, anyway, to look farther down the river.

The controversial fires of 1988 killed lots of wildlife in the Park. The big question was whether to adhere to Park policy and let nature take its course, which meant let the fires burn, or to intervene and fight them. Lots of years not letting nature take its course—not letting wildfires burn—had piled up an enormous amount of fuel, waiting for ignition during a drought. It came in a hot dry summer of 1988, and the Park burned for weeks before fires finally threatened buildings and firefighters stepped in to save them. The general reaction was outrage at the time, at letting so much go up in smoke. But now the new shoots of plants, springing up in sunlight let in by the fire, make much of the burned areas better habitat for animals, such as these mule deer, than it was before the burn. Dave Hughes

6

Buffalo Ford

At times anglers line up to fish the best holding water in the Buffalo Ford part of the river. But the fish are plentiful, the catch and release ethic keeps them that way. Masako Tani

◆

Facing page: Masako Tani proves the constant adage that if you where the right hat you'll catch the right fish, with a bright two-pound-plus cutthroat taken from the smooth waters of the Buffalo Ford reach of the Yellowstone. Dave Hughes

I sat in the cool grass with my wadered toes stretched almost to the edge of the swishing river, and was quite surprised to see a plump trout materialize in the water nearly at my feet. It poked into the shallow gravel, took something, then nosed on. Two more followed it. All three took up feeding stations twenty feet from me, visible in water no more than two feet deep, tails aquiver.

They began feeding with a ragged rhythm that included an occasional rise to take

something on top. I slowly lifted my miniature binoculars, focused into the feeding lane of the nearest trout. It rose. I scanned upstream its lane a ways, and spotted a tiny insect floating peacefully along, and followed it with the binoculars as it drifted down toward its death. The trout tipped up. The insect disappeared. At such close range it was easy to see that the innocent victim was a Little Olive mayfly, a *Baetis*.

Nobody else had noticed all this happening. I looked up and down the river. Quite a few anglers were in sight, some inexpert, flailing the water, some expert, setting flies onto the water with such delicacy that the flies looked around in surprise to see how they'd got there. Some anglers danced with bent rods, and I wasn't able to say for certain that the experts hooked fish more often than the beginners.

Folks fished in different ways: most nymphed, some tossed wets or streamers, a few fished dries. I wanted to take mine on top, so I stooped out of there without disturbing the three feeding trout, waded into position below them, and prepared to fish for them.

First I lengthened my tippet with about three feet of fine 6X leader. Then I patted myself down for the Sucrettes tin that is my *Baetis* box. I tied on a 18 Little Olive Compara-dun, dressed it with floatant, fluffed it with my fingers into the perfect mayfly shape. The nearest trout rose. I set the fly onto the water about three feet above the trout's lie. The little dry cocked itself nicely on the water, said, "Here I am," and strolled toward the trout. I crouched low and squinted into the water, wanting to see all the excitement as it unfolded.

All the excitement was simply this: the trout swam a couple of feet to the side, out from under the drift of my leader and fly, and took up a new feeding station.

I cast again; the trout moved over again. Before long I'd driven that fish right into deep water, where I could no longer see it, where it was no longer profitable for the fish to rise all the way to the top for a minuscule insect. I reeled up, examined the fly. It looked all right to me, but not to the fish. I replaced it with an olive Harrop Hairwing Dun in the same size. Then I looked toward the two remaining trout, which still rose despite the disturbance I'd made chasing their friend away.

This time I worked into position at an angle above the trout. When I cast, it was downstream with lots of slack in the line. As this slack fed out, the fly floated freely. It arrived ahead of the line and leader. The first trout rose up, backed down with the fly, took it with a swirl and shot off astonished when I set the hook. A few minutes later I kneeled in the shallows to unhook it, admired its golden colors, spanked its tail and watched it swim away. A little later I did the same with the second.

Cutthroat trout are supposed to be stupid, especially on the Buffalo Ford reach of the Yellowstone River. Sometimes they are. They drop down from the lake in June to spawn. That act absorbs all their energy and attention. They're hungry when it's over. When the reach of river opens to fishing July fifteenth, the cutts are eager to feed, and they can't afford to be selective. It's a marvelous time and place to be a beginner with a fly rod in your hand. Because the water is so clear, the trout so visible and so willing, you'll learn a lot about fly fishing in a hurry.

The same cutts get filled out fairly fast, and they also get a quick education about fishermen and flies. By the first of August they can already be damnably selective. You've got to lengthen your tippet, choose a fly that looks at least a little like the natural, and present it to the fish with a free float, without drag. However, you can combat all these difficulties by finding fish that haven't been pestered.

Catch-and-release is the rule on the most popular part of the river. This cutt is being slipped back into the water to finish out its natural life cycle: to spawn again, to fight again. Masako Tani

White pelicans cruise the river, improve the scenery, but interfere with the fishing at times, crashlanding without bashfulness right in the midst of a flock of anglers casting to selective trout, putting the fish down.
Dave Hughes

◆

Crafty coyote hunts a meadow alongside the river for mice and other rodents. Dave Hughes

The road runs right along the west bank of the river from the Upper Falls almost to Yellowstone Lake, more than ten miles upstream. But the far side has only a trail, with access at each end; there are no roads near it. The trail is well marked and easy, but surprisingly seldom traveled. If you get over to the other side, especially in July when the water is slightly high and the river is still difficult to wade across at Buffalo Ford, folks will look at you in wonder, puzzled about how *you* got there.

The stretch of water between the falls and the lake is eleven miles of the most beautiful trout water you'll ever see. The lake serves to even out flows from the mercurial upper river, and also to settle out its silt. The Buffalo Ford reach is like a giant spring creek, slightly high but very clear in July, falling and becoming easier to wade through August, September, and October. Its surroundings are magnificent. About half of it lies in Hayden Valley, and that half is closed forever to fishing, sanctuary for wildlife that ranges from ducks and geese to otters and elk. The most famous inhabitants of the valley are buffalo.

Hayden Valley was at one time part of the old lake bed. Then it got topped by an ice cap. The melting ice left glacial gravels of the valley impacted with clay, which doesn't drain well. The wet soil holds so much water that trees can't take root. So Hayden Valley is a swamp-meadow in the bottoms with grass and sagebrush slopes rolling away east and west of the meandering river. Herds of buffalo congregate in the open meadows mornings and evenings and drift away toward the shade of distant trees when the sun gets hot in the afternoon. The valley might be the nearest thing you'll ever see to nature the way it was before man forced it into a corner.

Masako and I spent some fruitless time on this part of the river. You should know about it so you don't chase around like we did. On a short visit, you can't afford to waste days.

What we did was try to get off to ourselves, and try to find trout in good numbers, all in a hectic hurry. We dashed up and down the road. We crossed Fishing Bridge at the lake and trotted far downstream on the trail, then turned around and trotted right back because a quick glance didn't reveal pods of feeding fish. Finally we got worn down. Masako went for a snooze in the car. I sat next to a popular stretch of stream in my waders, wondering why other folks held bent rods in their hands while I caught nothing but frustration. That's when those three trout surprised me by swimming over the gravel right in front of me, taking up feeding stations where it was easy to cast over them, though not necessarily so easy to catch them.

◆

Sleepy-eyed buffalo is the last one you want to walk up on; catch this old bull by surprise and he's liable to give chase. Despite their size, buffalo are surprisingly quick and agile. They can outrun you, and they far outweigh you. Stay away. Several people get hurt by buffalo in Yellowstone Park each year. Dave Hughes

Aerial view of Fishing Bridge shows the spring creek nature of the river below Yellowstone Lake, the most popular reach of river in the world, yet one that still provides remarkable fishing. Dave Hughes

It taught me something that we were able to apply over and over on the clear waters of the entire Yellowstone: relax, let the fish come to you. Pick a likely lie, take up a comfortable station, tip polaroids down over your nose, watch into the water for awhile. If you fall asleep, that's not a problem. Trout might be right in front of you when you wake up.

Yellowstone cuts are like mottled ghosts. They feed with minimum movement along the bottom and sometimes move to the top and take floating insects with quiet rises. Their presence won't jump right out at you. You've got to let it seep into you.

There's an extreme advantage to spotting fish from a quiet position. When you find them, they'll be feeding confidently. Because you're already there, they won't be alarmed by your arrival. I've hiked the banks and seen fish that spotted me before I noticed them. They freeze into near invisibility, or drift under a cut bank, or dash out of the area altogether. Even when I've been able to pin down their location, and make perfect presentations to them, they rarely take once they've been alerted to my presence. This gets to be a larger truth as the season proceeds and the fish have seen more anglers.

This eleven miles of river meanders gently over its impacted clay bottom, with very few riffles. Its current is forceful but also predictable. Weeds wave in the current and grow longer beards as the season goes on. Wading would be easy except that the bottom is deceptive. Potholes and sudden drops get hidden in those weedbeds. It's easy to step into one, not so easy to step back out.

The river is eternally cold because it feeds out of the deep lake. It is best not to fall in, but helpful to be wearing neoprene waders if you do. They're the best safety device I know about for two reasons: first, they'll keep you warm and afloat if you do fall into the water, and second, they're so hot when you're out of the water that they discourage you from chasing after buffalo. I'm not sure which is most important. Don't chase buffalo no matter what kind of waders you wear. It can get terribly painful if they decide to turn around and chase you back.

We nearly found out one day, or so I think. Masako wanted a close-up photo of an old bull drowsing in a dust bed just above the river. She approached to within about fifty feet, clicking away, not experienced with wild animals so not aware of any danger. I followed her, restraining her, trying to gauge the old bull's worry distance, suddenly realizing that it couldn't be gauged because the bull was asleep.

Masako started to step closer to the bull. I tugged her back and the huge bull jumped nimbly to its feet all in the same instant. The bull looked at us balefully for a moment, then dropped its head and began eating grass.

Another danger, this one concealed, lies at the lower end of this placid part of the river. The water begins to get slightly urgent where it turns the last corner and passes under a bridge. Then it suddenly rushes down a chute toward the upper falls. If you think that would be a minor whirl, take a hike down the trail to enjoy the view of the falls, then judge how far above the bridge you'd like to fish, and how carefully you'd like to wade, in order to avoid that trip. A few unfortunate fishermen have taken it in the past, but none have described it. Fish far above the bridge and don't take any wading chances when you fish above the falls.

Successful methods for the Buffalo Ford reach are not at all like what works on the river above the lake, or in the lake itself. Streamers and wet flies work wonders up there. Down in this rich part of the river trout feed on aquatic insects that emerge out of the weedbeds. These are usually small, and most often must be imitated with small dry flies and nymphs.

Standard nymphs work well. Try Hare's Ears, Zug Bugs, Muskrats, and Pheasant Tails, all in sizes 12 to 16. That covers the color spectrum of naturals well. But don't just toss them out and fish them at random. Try to get them down toward the bottom, which is where trout feed on nymphs most of the time. You can use a wet-tip line to accomplish this. Masako and I watched a fellow fishing nymphs this way in late July. He surprised an abundance of fish.

He fished the roaded side of the river, but on a bend far enough from the road that few people cared to join him. We did, but discovered that where he waded the water was too deep and had too many treacherous potholes to dare launching light Masako into it. We waded in at the edges, watched him fish, duplicated his tactics. It netted us a couple of trout. But his count got up to around thirty or forty before we left in distress.

The way this bold wader fished was simple. He tiptoed around potholes and threaded his way out waist deep, tied a weighted nymph to a fast sinking wet-tip line and cast it out slightly upstream. As it reached a point straight out from his position, it also reached the bottom. He let it tumble along as far as it would go without rising from the bottom. Then he brought it up and cast again. But most of the time a trout intercepted it while it was down there.

Most people fish nymphs on a standard split-shot-and-indicator setup. This is easy to master once you learn to cast an open loop so all the gadgets on your leader don't tangle. The setup is simple: use a floating line, an eight to ten foot leader, and slip a bright strike indicator about two-thirds of the way up the leader toward the line tip. Then tie your nymph to a short tippet: eight to ten inches. Clamp a small split shot or two above the tippet knot. The knot will keep the shot from sliding down to pal with the nymph.

Your cast should be upstream at an angle across the currents. Toss line in upstream mends if you have to, in order to give the indicator a free float. The nymph will plummet directly to the bottom and drift idly along there. If you're fishing right the indicator will hesitate once in a while. It could be bottom; it could be a fish. Either way, you've got to set the hook to be sure. If you're not hitting bottom now and then, or catching a fish, add another shot.

The key to this kind of nymphing is depth. I'm constantly amazed how often I fish totally barren water, then add an extra shot and discover that the water is suddenly full of fish. It's disappointing if you've spent a couple of hours casting before adding that next split shot.

Successful dry fly fishing at Buffalo Ford holds fewer secrets because things happen up where you can see them. The first thing to try to see is the natural insect trout are taking, if you can catch one. I always carry a dollar aquarium net in my vest, so I can dip it into the currents and hoist a mayfly or midge in its meshes.

Most of the time you'll capture a small mayfly. There are some Gray Drakes (*Siphlonurus*) and Green Drakes (*Ephemerella*) that arrive in size 12. More often you'll fish over size 16 and 18 Little Olives (*Baetis*), size 20 and 22 Tricos (*Tricorythodes*), size 16 and 18 Pale Morning Duns or size 14 and 16 Blue-wing Olives (both *Ephemerella* species). Your dry fly boxes should reflect such expectations. Fly shops in Livingston, Gardiner, and West Yellowstone can all inform you about current hatches, and help you arm yourself to match them.

Tactics should deviate by several degrees from the standard

upstream dry fly presentation. The reason lies in those smooth and clear currents: a line, leader, and fly cast straight upstream will fly right over the fish. If that doesn't frighten them, the leader and line drifting down ahead of the fly will put them off their feed and sometimes cause them to move over a couple of feet to get out of harm's way, as happened to me.

One solution is to move slightly off to the side, cast upstream, but without lining the fish. This will often fool them. A second solution is to move directly across the current from the fish, cast just above them and let the fly drift down to them. It helps to use a reach cast, leaning over upstream as the line lights on the water, then following it downstream, giving the fly a free float. A third solution is to do what I did after I'd chased the first of those three trout into deep water. I moved upstream and then cast down to the fish with slack in the line to feed into the drift of the fly. The slack is achieved simply by wobbling the rod while the line is still in the air. It lands on the water like a snake out for a swim, in a series of S-turns.

The Buffalo Ford reach got its name because the centerpiece of the system is a shallow ford where buffalo cross the river. When the water is down a bit, from late August on, you can cross there, too, opening up lots of the far shore to easy access. But buffalo can cross just about any place they hit the river.

Masako and I watched a couple of them tackle the river just downstream from the easy ford. They waded in powerfully. I was jealous: if I could wade like that I could fish where you could not. When the water rose onto their shoulders, they swam ponderously, drifting downstream but never picking up the pace or panicking. When their feet struck bottom again they took up wading again, shouldering against the current, pushing up white waves. They arrived at a steep, undercut bank. They waded to the base of it, then patiently pawed at it until they'd worn a gash in it, and plodded powerfully up the gash as if it were a trail into the trees.

After their passing, it was a trail.

That propensity to wade the river wherever they hit it must cost lots of buffalo their lives.

A typical three-pound Yellowstone cutthroat from the Buffalo Ford part of the river. Note the tiny dry fly in its upper lip, proof that these fish are not always as stupid as they're reputed to be. Dave Hughes

7

The
Invisible
River

A pretty cutthroat from the Black Canyon that fell for a Deer Hair Caddis fished tight against bankside boulders. Dave Hughes

Facing page: The river is big and pushy in the Black Canyon. It doesn't give you much room for wading, though you can often nibble at its fish along its edges. Dave Hughes

A river shows its youth in its canyons. The recurrent eruptions of the last two million years laid down great layers of rhyolite lava in the Canyon Village area of Yellowstone Park. Intermittent ice caps locked the river during the Ice Ages, retarded cutting its new course. Ground water, heated by the nearness of the massive magma pool still cooking under parts of the Yellowstone Plateau, filtered up through the rhyolites, leached the lavas and weakened them.

When the ice retreated, the river sliced through these soft rhyolites like a knife. The result is the Grand Canyon of the Yellowstone, between Canyon Village and Tower. The leached lava flows are visible from overlooks at Upper and Lower Falls; they are odd shades of yellow and red. Slender columns stand tall as buildings on the pitched canyon walls, where hard stone caps protected the softer rock from erosion while all the rock around it got whisked away. These columns still wear their protective caps like berets.

The reason for the sharp cut of the Grand Canyon is the rhyolite flows softened and colored by the leachings of steam percolating up out of the ground from the hot ground water just beneath the surface of the earth. Scott Ripley

The falls mark the point where the river dives over the edge of hard lava flows, into those softer flows where ground water leached out minerals and softened the lava.

The Grand Canyon is about fifteen miles long, steeply walled, with access points at either end and not much chance to reach the river in between. Most places, you'd have to go down on ropes. You couldn't move very far up and down the river once you got there; sheer walls drop too often into violent water. But the trail at Tower, at the lower end of the Grand Canyon, drops swiftly to the river and gives access upstream to about three or four miles.

This is bank water, with the depths lapping right to the edges. Go down in shorts and rock-hopping shoes. At least on exploratory trips you can leave your waders behind.

The Grand Canyon is above the entrance of the Lamar River, and is clear all spring. When salmonfly nymphs get restless and migrate toward shore for emergence, they draw trout in with them. The river in the canyon opens to fishing Memorial Day weekend. Fishing is best from that time until the salmonfly hatch ends in late July. Then the trout move back out into deeper water. It's tough to reach them because the water is too deep and swift and treacherous to wade.

The Black Canyon takes the river the next twenty miles on its westward curve toward Gardiner and its exit from the Park.

The geography here is a combination of lava flows and old granite. Thermal activity that softened the rock in the Grand Canyon didn't work its way this far north, so the river has eroded a more normal, less brutal, course. But it is still eroded sharply into this young country.

Access to the Black Canyon is easier. Where the highway bridge crosses the river near Roosevelt, you can hike upstream and down. From the bridge you can view the last of the thermal workings on the rock of the upper canyon. Look upstream and you'll see steam vents and yellow rock: weakened rhyolites. Downstream the rock firms up, the canyon changes.

A trail follows the entire length of the Black Canyon, from Roosevelt to Gardiner. Unlike the trail along the Grand Canyon, it is not perched high on the rim, pitched directly above the river far below. Instead, it follows the river, sometimes just above the banks, other times climbing up tumbled scree slopes, but at times even touching the river. The entire Black Canyon is far from the road except at its upper and lower ends. You can get into it, and fish it nicely, on day hikes at those ends. The fishing is just as good there, and almost as lonely, as it is in the center of the canyon, far removed from any access. But to see the whole of it you've got to backpack through it.

My nephew Trevor and I decided that's what we'd do. We set up a schedule for a three day trip, six miles a day, hitting the river at Hellroaring Creek, just downstream from Roosevelt bridge, hiking to Gardiner. It was late August; we had no trouble getting permits for the camps we wanted. Not many people wanted to be on the river then.

It's best to fish this canyon part of the Yellowstone earlier. Salmonflies hatch in the first three weeks of July most years. If runoff ends early, you can fish the canyons the first or second week. If the river is still high the Black Canyon will be discolored by the muddied outflow of the Lamar River, which joins the Yellowstone at the junction of the Grand and Black Canyons. The best time to fish the Black Canyon, then, is in the week or two just at the end of runoff, as early as you can. But we had to go when we could, so we went in August.

We carried Halazone tablets to purify our water. Because buffalo plop so much dung upstream, you've got to have some way to kill bacteria and parasites downstream. Boiling the water is fine; just be sure to take lots of fuel for your backpacking stove. Open fires are not allowed in this part of the canyon, so you can't boil your water over a campfire.

Prickly pear cactus is beautiful when it's in bloom. Most of the time it is hidden in the grass and very damaging when you whack it with hand or foot. Masako Tani

◆

The Hellroaring Trail down to the river is steep. Trevor and I dropped straight down through burnt country to cross the Yellowstone on a footbridge. Looking down from the bridge, it's easy to see why the river is not fished much in its canyons. The river that flows one hundred yards wide in the Buffalo Ford reach is constricted to ten yards between tall walls in parts of the Black Canyon. You would not fish it; you could not fish it. We trudged on across a wide sage flat, watched thunderstorms play above the canyon, tried to calculate their trajectories.

For the rest of that first six mile day, we were a couple of contour lines above the river, looking down, getting an occasional glimpse of the glint of it through trees. But in late afternoon we dropped down suddenly to our first camp, and found ourselves on a flat in what might be the most beautiful part of the river I'd yet seen. It was wide between grassed and sloping banks, featured with boulders, deep and green in places, flat and shallow in others. It looked promising for fishing, but the promise was only slightly fulfilled.

I fixed a quick dinner over the Whisperlite: two packages of boiled noodles mixed with a chicken gravy packet and a can of

canned chicken. Trevor, the chronic teenager, surprised me and said it was good. Then he drew the backpacks high into the air on a bear pole, out of harm's way, and we went fishing.

Trevor fished the run in front of the tent. I hiked upstream through the grass meadow and watched the river for rises. I didn't see any, but spotted a fine flat, so started to descend the steep bank. A rock rolled out from under my feet, I stabbed my left hand to the ground to catch myself, and was hit by a swift stinging pain. I'd been struck by a snake.

The snake was a prickly pear cactus. My hand landed on it and broke several lobes away. They stuck in my hand. My fingers were massed with spines and bleeding. I pried the lobes of cactus off my flesh with the blade of a Swiss Army knife. Then I sat for fifteen minutes and picked out spines with the knife's tweezers. In the following weeks spines that I could not remove worked their way through my hand and fingers like worms. One broke the protective sheath around the knuckle of my index finger and left it sore and inflamed for more than two months. It would have been worse without those tweezers. I'll never go backpacking again without that red knife in my pocket.

I got distracted from my pain by the discovery that fish were rising all over the flat in front of me.

◆

Lots of places in the beautiful Black Canyon hold trout, from the look of them, but you could never get down to fish these places and prove it. Dave Hughes

Grasshoppers become a major food source for trout. . .and for coyotes and songbirds and even hawks, for that matter. Dave Hughes

They were whitefish. I took several on an Elk Hair Caddis dry. Then Trevor worked his way up along the bank to the flat, and I watched him take several fish on the same dry fly. It was his first success with the floating fly. He learned quickly to get a good drift, follow the float of the fly, raise the rod to a take, bring the fish in and subdue all the squirmings of it, unhook it and release it.

The next day we hiked our six miles in hot sun, hectored by mosquitoes. When we walked through tall grass and sage, so many grasshoppers kicked out ahead of us that they looked like wading waves. They flew in all directions, some thudding against our bare chests as we hiked.

Whenever we stopped to rest I tossed hopper patterns along the banks. Only a couple of trout speared up to take them. They were cutts, pretty, but not as large as those in the lake or at Buffalo Ford. I wondered what kind of trout had lurked along those banks earlier, when salmonfly nymphs crawled to shore there and drew trout out of the depths behind them. Most trout were back down in the depths, where I couldn't get at them.

I did do some damage with nymphs, fishing them deep on a split shot and strike indicator. But most of the damage was to whitefish, which caused me to quit fishing and saddle up again and head through the heat toward the next camp.

We reached our campsite early that afternoon, set the tent, and rolled out sleeping bags. Trevor, worn out by the unfamiliar weight of his heavy pack, took a snooze. I picked up my fly rod, wandered upstream, and found a gorgeous broad flat just above camp. It was shallow, with clear water and clean bottom stones. I rigged a size 16 Fox Squirrel nymph below two light split shot and fixed a small strike indicator about four feet up the leader. It looked like an excellent place to exercise the casting stroke, to let cool water on bare legs wash away the day's difficulty, to let the isolation of the canyon seep in, to let the wildness have its way with me.

It didn't work. My drowsy thoughts were constantly interrupted by the dipping of the indicator. The flat was massed with fish, but again they were whitefish. It was a perfect tutorial in this critical nymph fishing technique. Since I've never quite conquered the method, I cast and caught fish until the calves of my legs went numb.

Facing page: Lower Falls plunges 308 feet over the edge of a hardened lava flow and the river begins to erode its sharp course through the softened rhyolites of the Grand Canyon. Masako Tani

Trevor joined me. I sat in the grass at streamside and watched him wade the flat, getting a similar degree of education in the dry fly method. That single evening might have propelled him years along the path toward excellence in fly fishing.

At dark I left Trevor fishing and started through the sage and grass toward the trail, a hundred feet up. As I walked I thought, "If this was the Deschutes, I'd be watching for snakes on this kind of ground." Usually such thoughts are protection against bad outcomes. You don't get struck by lightning when you are thinking about getting struck by lightning, do you?

The canyon reaches of the river, and of course all of the water down in the lower elevations, is home to this fellow by whom you don't want to get surprised. Be watchful whenever hiking or fishing in rocky or brushy areas. Ben O. Williams

I didn't get struck by the snake, but I heard the thump as it jumped out of my path. A rattlesnake has weight; it can swing its front half on the pivot of its back half, to get its head and what I guess what you might call its chest out of the way of a striding beast. When it makes that swing you can sometimes hear the thump of its front half landing. You've heard so much about the rattlesnakes rear end warning system and how you'll never mistake it for anything else. I don't find that true for my ears, which are not good ones. I confuse grasshoppers for rattlers, and what's not so smart, confuse rattlers for grasshoppers. But I've never confused the thump of a snake for the landing of a hopper. I leaped.

The snake was not so near, five feet away, coiled, cocked, quivering. I backed up, made a wide swing around it, and headed on toward the trail. I called out to Trevor, "Watch where you're walking. There's rattlers up here."

"You see one?" he hollered.

"Right here," I shouted back.

Trevor heeded my warning about watching where to walk by reeling up, thrashing out of the water, and tearing through the grass and sage to see the snake. I didn't know he'd never seen one. I'd lost sight of it by then, and it must have gone down a hole. He never did find it, though the next day we found another sleeping in the backpack trail in the mid-day sun. It caused another leap, and Trevor got to see his snake.

That last day we also saw one lone fisherman pitching flies from the bank. We stood on the trail right above him and watched him fish. He was not aware of our presence, and we didn't inform him about it, instead letting him enjoy his sense of having the entire canyon to himself.

He was the only other fisherman we saw on the trip through the Black Canyon.

The Lamar System

Whenever heavy rain hits the Park, the Lamar River announces its entrance into the Yellowstone rather loudly: it's an influx of mud. The upper Lamar and some of its tributaries have fine silt beds on the slopes above them. Thunderstorms, occurring nearly daily in July and August, set this silt sliding down the banks, send it sailing down the streams and dump it into the Yellowstone River near Tower Junction. It can render Paradise Valley and even the lower river unfishable for days during the peak of the fishing season.

It is one of the reasons you want to have lots of fallback options in mind when planning a trip to Yellowstone country.

One of the finest options is Slough Creek, a tributary to the Lamar River that does not often muddy up. You can fish lower Slough Creek from the road that follows it up to the campground. You won't find a prettier place in the Park. This part of Slough Creek has open sagebrush banks, with aspen groves on the rolling hills high above the stream. The roaded part gets hit hard. Its trout have PhD degrees in entomology and teach fly fishing courses in local fly shops. Hoppers are their most common fare, but daily doses of mayflies are also on the menu.

You've got to tramp to see the best parts of Slough Creek. It's a two-mile hike, uphill, to the first meadow. Beyond that a succession of rapids and then meadows escort you upward as far as you'd care to go, but you've got to camp to enjoy them.

Masako and I made the two-mile hike to the first meadow one afternoon and encountered surprising beauty and exceptional fishing. The beauty came atop a granite butte in the center of the meadow, where a mule deer doe and her two fawns got to their feet, wiggled their long tails and ears, stepped off daintily and

Preceding page: Tributaries to the Yellowstone River, such as Slough Creek in the Lamar System, offer fishing that is excellent, sometimes lonely, and often supurb at times when the Yellowstone itself is out of shape because of snowmelt or runoff from thunderstorms. Dave Hughes

A beautiful, bright gold Slough Creek cutthroat. Masako Tani

View of the first meadow of Slough Creek from the butte that stands above it. It's a beautiful piece of water, separated from the road by a couple of miles of uphill hiking, therefore slightly less crowded and slightly easier fishing than the lower stream. Masako Tani

A herd of buffalo crosses the glacial valley of the Lamar River. Dave Hughes

Wetting a line on some of the smaller waters in the Park is an excellent way to get away from the crowds, get into some beautiful places that tourists don't see from the highways. Dave Hughes

began nibbling bitterbrush. They were not alarmed by our presence, and I thought about the innocence of all those vast herds of animals that roamed our plains when man first arrived.

We had no trouble finding rising trout to work over. We did have some trouble coaxing them to our flies. They wouldn't take hopper dressings, though grasshoppers leaped and flew through the grasses. Finally I noticed tiny mayflies hatching. We tied on appropriate imitations and started fooling some fish. They were pure strain Yellowstone cutts, and averaged sixteen inches long. One weighed well over two pounds.

I wouldn't advise hiking into the first meadow to avoid other anglers and find easy fishing. That happens on Slough Creek, but farther up. If you fish the lower end by the campground, or just the first meadow, you'll see people, and the fish will be far from foolish. Hike to the second meadow and higher and you'll start to feel lonely and find some fish that are easy.

The Lamar River itself is a wonder when it's in shape. It flows through a vast open valley, carved by a glacier. Herds of buffalo snort, bellow, roll in the dust. The river is full of willing trout, all cutthroat. It's not fished hard, so they rise to dries that aren't anatomically correct.

The Lamar flows for miles through a broad plain. The road follows it, but in many places the river is a mile away, on the far side of the valley. You won't find many people fishing over there. But before you make the hike, check the river out where the road crosses it down below. If it's muddied up, don't bother. This isn't idle advice; the Lamar is dirty a high percentage of the summer.

The road departs and the Lamar River flows up into its glacial canyon for miles through beautiful country that you must hike to see. It's a backpacker's show; you won't have much company if you decide to fish it. But you run the risk that the river will go out every time a violent thunderstorm strikes.

In Yellowstone country, that is often.

8

Paradise

A beautiful Paradise Valley brown trout that made its mistake on a salmonfly nymph fished along the bottom of the Yellowstone River. Scott Ripley

◆

Facing page: The rugged Beartooth Mountains form the eastern uplift above the Yellowstone River and its pastoral landscape in Paradise Valley. Ben O. Williams

Rick Smith is a Yellowstone River guide out of Bozeman. Skip Gibson is a tackle rep for Dan Bailey's wholesale operation out of Livingston. They took me down the river in an Avon drifter one early day in May. The weather went through all the contortions typical for a time that's still on the border of winter: rain and wind, snow and hail, calm and warm sunshine. While waiting to launch, shivering and dancing with hands in my pockets, I was unable to under- stand Rick and Skip's enthusiasm. By the end of the day, it was all explained.

The river was low and clear. Our first stop was at a shallow backchannel where some tat- tered foam swizzled in a lazy eddy. I wondered why we stopped there, waded without thought right up to the eddy, and suddenly saw something dimpling the foam from beneath. I peered more closely. It was noses of trout pok- ing at midges. I backed up, tied on a size 16 Adams and set it on the foam. It rode there a moment. Then a nose poked out of the foam and the fly disappeared.

I swept the rod high to set the hook, expecting to come back against a tiddler, wanting to skid it out of there fast so it wouldn't disturb the others. It was a mistake. My fine tippet snapped. A rainbow leaped into the air and looked around to see what had stung it. I could see my fly pinned in its lip as the trout hovered in front of me. That fish would have gone a couple of pounds, but I was never going to heft it in my hands to find out exactly what it weighed.

It fell back to the water with a whap, then flapped into the air a couple more times, spooking the rest of the trout out of the eddy. I reeled up and waded out swearing at myself. But it didn't take Rick long to find more fish.

We passed them in the boat, just a couple rising softly in a slick a hundred yards upstream from a classic Yellowstone riffle, where an island split the river. Rick parked the boat at the head of the island. Skip bounded out to dance with some trout in the riffle corner. Rick dashed off to explore the backchannel behind the island. Rising trout always set the spurs to me, so I galloped upstream in a shower of spray toward that slick.

Moth finds its morning rest on the open petals of a primrose alongside the river. Dave Hughes

◆

When I arrived the first thing I did was sit on a boulder, catch my breath, and watch the water. As always, the two fish I'd seen turned into a scattered half dozen or so. They fed sporadically on insects that broke through the surface of the slick, rode the still current for a few feet, then lifted into the air to fly away if no noses arose to finish them first. I thought they were the same midges I'd seen in the eddy. I tried to capture one but couldn't, so settled for observing one through my miniature binoculars. It was a caddis, dark brown almost to black, about a size 18. Its life ended even as I watched. I vowed to save some others.

The nearest thing I had to the natural was a size 16 Deer Hair Caddis. I tied one on. Wading the slick would have flushed all the fish, so I kneeled at its edge, made my casts from there, and set the fly onto the water as softly as I could. It worked. A trout rose confidently to the fly. I set the hook softly, played the fish gently, without regard to how it might spook the others. This sent them all to flight, but I landed it, which made it worth it.

The trout was a cutthroat, agleam on its cheeks, gold down its flanks, spotted on its tail. It was about fourteen inches long, plump as a healthy maiden. I would have released it even if the law had not required it. Cutts are protected in Paradise Valley.

Paradise extends from the boundary of the Park, at Gardiner, nearly sixty miles north to Livingston. The valley is the basin at the foot of the faults that rise up to form the Beartooths and Absarokas. The riverbottom is broad and flat. The mountains tower abruptly above it to the east, in a long uplifted line that allows little entry into some of the most forbidding country in the world. When you fish the river in Paradise Valley those looming mountains are a constant presence, always hanging over your shoulder. In May they're still white with snow.

After releasing the cutthroat I moved upstream a few yards and found a small break where the water rounded a point and left a slight swirl in its wake. A trout rose daintily there, taking the same caddis. I dropped the fly onto the eddy, the fish came to it quickly, and I raised the rod abruptly to surprise it. The fish dashed out into the flat, jumped twice, then came reluctantly to my hand. It was a brown, dark on its cheeks, nearly the gold of a cutthroat on its sides, but with big black spots surrounded by soft red haloes. It was a longer fish than the earlier cutt, perhaps sixteen inches, but not so heavy in my hand.

◆

Lourde's Shrine near Emigrant stands beautifully next to the river, with the Beartooths in the background. Dave Hughes

I saw Rick waving at me as I slipped the brown back into the water. "Come down here!" he hollered. So I galloped back.

Rick had found a pod of trout rising in a cutbank pool in the backchannel behind the island. The pool was about sixty feet wide. The trout rose greedily against the far bank, where the current was strongest. The water nearly seethed with them. Rick already had everything figured out for me. "They're taking *Baetis* mayflies. Try a number sixteen olive dry." I searched my boxes, found a couple of Harrop Hairwing Duns, tied one on. I waded out and found I could only get about ten feet from shore before the water dropped away.

The pool required a fifty foot cast with slack line at its end for a perfect float. The wind snorted downstream. The fly was a size 16, lost at long range among many naturals the same size. My casts were not often perfect, and the trout were picky. But when the line lit right and the fly discovered itself floating naturally down the current, the results were predictable. Rick managed to hold them in his hands more often than I did. They were rainbows, between one and two pounds.

We wound up so sated by day's end that we floated along in the raft and watched rising trout without even casting to them. We'd taken three species, cutts, browns, and rainbows, plus more whitefish than you'd care to count. Most of our fishing was on dries, but Skip, who's an expert with nymphs, fished the indicator and shot method for awhile, and alarmed so many trout that we became alarmed ourselves.

In the following days the Mother's Day Caddis hatch increased until it dominated everything. The insects floated down the river just like we did: in rafts. Trout rose to scoop them by the mouthful. The difficulty was to separate a drifting dry fly from all those naturals, to detect a take.

Sylvester Nemes was the one to solve it. He's the author of *The Soft-Hackled Fly*. He lives in Bozeman, prowls the Yellowstone in spring. His pattern for the Mother's Day Caddis is a wet fly fished sub-surface. It's a brilliant idea. You don't have to see the fly to notice a take. You're able to feel it. And the trout are perfectly satisfied to make it all happen just the way Syl says it will: sometimes with a soft pull, other times with a thump.

Temperatures that incite the caddisflies to riot also prompt the annual snowmelt to begin up in the headwaters. The river perches on the edge of its spring flood. You get a week of excellent fishing, arriving at the river every day to drift it or fish the banks. Then one day you drive over Carter's Bridge, look down at the river, and behold water the color and nearly the consistency of pecan fudge. It is full of debris, limbs, even cottonwood trees. You shake your head sadly. Paradise Valley is going to be out for weeks.

In a normal year, it won't be fishable again until early July. If the year is not normal, and the river clears by late June, you'll get to hit the salmonfly and green drake mayfly hatches. But most of the time you get in on the tail end of these, and the river gets hot during the hopper hatch.

The Yellowstone River in Paradise Valley is one of the most beautiful places in the world when the cottonwood leaves turn yellow and begin to fall.
Dave Hughes

Congregations of salmonflies gather along the banks of the river in early July. In those years when the water is clear and fishable then, with the runoff ending early, you can get some quarrelsome action from the trout by plopping a big imitation right to the edge of the river. Ben O. Williams

Of course, it's not a hatch. It's a windfall. Grasshoppers live on land, launch themselves into the air with strong legs and little forethought about where they're going to land. If one springs up near the river and the wind is blowing, the insect is in for a surprise and some trout is in for a meal. The wind does blow in Paradise Valley.

I'll tell you why. The air in the mountains to the south is constantly cool. The air on the plains to the north gets hot. Hot air rises; cool air collapses. When the hot air rises off the plains every afternoon, the cool air in the mountains rushes down to take its place. This happens everywhere. What doesn't happen everywhere is that the rush of cool air gets constricted in Paradise Valley, then is forced to breach the cramped gap at Livingston. The wind blows there, which is stating it faintly.

You want to fish a seven- or eight-weight rod during terrestrial time on the Yellowstone River. If you fish a four- weight the wind will boss your fly around. The fly should be big, a size 6 or 8, and you should paste it right to water that purls deeply along the banks. You can do this by rock-hopping along shore. You'll catch some fish, and they'll be nice ones. But you won't be able to cover much water, and trout are sprinkled lightly along the banks at this time of year. The more water you can cover, the more happiness you'll find.

That's why most guides float long stretches on summer days, covering ten to twenty miles of river rather than four or five. A float is an excellent way to combine some pleasant fishing with a lot of sight-seeing: getting escorted down the river by the current, the view unfolding for you.

Lots of hatches happen throughout the entire summer in Paradise Valley. If you prefer fishing them you won't be disappointed on many days. You'll find rising trout, most of them feeding on a variety of small mayflies, caddisflies, and midges.

Some of these hatches continue on into fall, and it becomes one of the most beautiful times to be on the Paradise Valley part of the river. The days begin to shorten up. The average weather is a high bright sun over the vast Montana sky. But storms do set in during September, and it's possible to spend three or four days under a sky that's not high and bright.

Masako and I spent three September days camped at Mallard's Rest in the center of the valley, floating the river each day. I made a mistake and pitched the tent where everybody else had pitched tents in the same campsite all summer, leaving the grass flattened. It was in the tiniest of hollows, a beautiful spot, the ground sloping downhill in all directions toward the tent. The weather didn't act like summer when we were there. Parts of each day it was nice. I did the morning shuttles on a mountain bike, after launching the boat.

Fishing was fine. Few fish rose, but nymphing took the fly down to them. Standard dressings worked well: Hare's Ears, Fox Squirrels, Muskrats. Cast with split shot on the leader a foot up, and an indicator a couple of times the depth of the water, these produced lots of trout. Most were holding at riffle corners, down the length of riffles, or in shallow runs. They had backed away from the banks where they staked out territories during the earlier terrestrial days.

On the last float of our trip the weather suddenly bucked up and snorted. Rain beat down in giant drops. Masako pulled the hood of her slicker over her head, hunched forward on her seat, and gave up fishing. I kept on fishing, but finally gave it up myself and urged the boat on with the wind, hurrying to the takeout in early afternoon. We returned to camp to find our sleeping bags wet, the pads beneath them soggy and heavy. Water had seeped right through the tent floor. We laughed as we rolled the pads and water squirted out.

◆

The tiny church at Meditation Point is a contemplative place alongside the river, a reassurance to travelers, whether they drive by on the highway or float by on the river itself. Dave Hughes

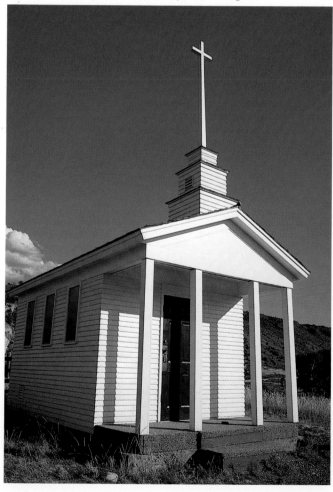

Gap in the anticline just above Livingston, where the Yellowstone River emerges from Paradise Valley, with the Beartooth Mountains in the background. This would have been the location of the dam proposed on the river for many years, a proposal defeated in the 1970s, and hopefully dead for all time. Dave Hughes

We'd already made reservations at Chico Hot Springs. As we drove up the river thirty miles to the hotel, the rain got angrier, soon became snow, which made us feel smarter about our reservations. That evening we soaked our bones for hours in the hot pools, then had a dinner that let us know why all the gourmet magazine editors lose the restraints on their language when they write about the place. It was truly an excellent way to end a fall trip in Paradise.

Later, in October, the weather returns to the big bright sky Montana is supposed to offer, though there is the chance of a true winter storm. But October is briefly the most beautiful time of year in Paradise Valley. The massed cottonwood bottoms flash into bright yellow. Geese move in from the north and gather at the same riffle corners you want to stop and fish. Deer begin to prowl more openly, and you see bands of them along the river. Most are mulies, with tall ears and black tails. But a few are whitetails, their horns slanted forward and their tails flapping when they run.

Big trout get restless in October, moving out of their sanctified depths onto riffles, where it's possible to swing a streamer in front of outsized noses. Sometimes they'll take. This is the best time of year to catch the brown of a lifetime. You're almost sure to take fish in the two to three pound class, trout that it's easy to be proud about. But bigger trout are taken often up and down the river.

On my October floats I tend to get lazy, to lay back on the oars and let the scenery unfold. I like to stalk deer on the islands, even though I carry no rifle. I like to watch geese, though I always try to keep on the far side of the river, to pass in the boat without

sending them into flight. Most of the time they go gronking off, not knowing that I've long ago removed myself from their list of enemies.

I'm less an enemy to the trout, too, at that time of year. I know it's time to arm a big rod with a heavy streamer, to step into the heavy water, to cast constantly and with great determination, swinging the fly through as much water as I can. But I don't do it anymore. I've left lots of big ones out there in Paradise Valley for you to catch.

Adult goose stands watchfully over its drowsing brood alongside the river in Paradise Valley. Ben O. Williams

Paradise Valley Spring Creeks

We all owe Bob Auger admiration and affection. In the late 1970s he left a landscaping business in New England and moved with his children to Paradise Valley. In the early 1980s he went to work on DePuy's Spring Creek, a degraded, dried up system that supported a small population of trout, a large population of handsome suckers, and an overpopulation of graceful but destructive mute swans.

Bob's speech is articulate. His hands are strong. I looked at them as we chatted in the fishing hut and believed it when he told me he'd dug some ditches at DePuys. The first ditch diverted lower Armstrong Spring Creek into a three-and-a-half mile dry streambed, converting the bed to a rich spring creek, ideal for spawning. The second ditch opened up a mile long channel too small for fishing, but not too small for spawning and rearing. The third thing he couldn't dig by hand.

It was a steam engine boiler, buried at the lower end of the old creekbed for a culvert into the Yellowstone River. It tapered from eight feet wide at one end to seven feet at the other. That's not much taper, but it was enough to accelerate water flowing through it so that few trout could swim against it. The boiler blocked access from the Yellowstone River to all that new spawning potential in DePuy's Spring Creek. It cost $22,000 to remove the boiler and replace it. The weight of it tipped two Monster Machines on their noses, but they got it out.

Trout now swim up out of the Yellowstone to spawn in nearly five miles of excellent water. DePuys and Armstrongs spring creeks both benefit from the surge of adult fish from the river. But the river itself receives a resurgence of fine fry each spawning season. Even if you don't fish the spring creeks, when you fish the main river you'll catch trout that originated there.

Transplanted trumpeter swan at its new home alongside DePuy's Spring Creek, part of the comeback for this great species. Ben O. Williams

---

Even bitter weather fails to stop the fish from rising, and the fishermen from trying for them, on the Paradise Valley spring creeks. Ben O. Williams

Bob Auger with the giant tapered steam boiler that served as a conduit for water leaving Depuy's Spring Creek. It accelerated the flow and blocked trout trying to get into the creek from the Yellowstone. When Bob removed it, several miles of spawning and rearing habitat was opened up. Dave Hughes

The clean-up at DePuys goes on. Bob strung seven miles of fence to keep cattle out of the water, removed old barb wire from the streambed, extracted dripping sheep fences, tires, car bodies, junk piles, and railroad ties. He's added deflection cribbings to create new holding lies, planted grass species that stabilize the banks. He's removed the mute swams, but brought in a few endangered trumpeters to help in their comeback.

With the renewal of DePuys, Paradise Valley now has three spring creeks that can be fished on a pay-per-day basis. Armstrong flows into DePuys, and was at one time the entirety of the system on the west side of the river, but is now the upper third of it. Its water is bright, beautiful; its trout are hefty, selective. Its hatches are wonderful. You don't want to fish here unless you want the challenge of matching a hatch.

Nelson's Spring Creek slips toward the Yellowstone from the east side of the river. It offers challenging water that pools nearly to stillness, and is in parts almost like a pond. Its fish have broad shoulders and are used to taking small insects and avoiding fishermens' flies. They are difficult, but so abundant that you'll spend the entire day casting over fish that are willing to take if you're able to get the right fly to them in the right way.

The trout in all three spring creeks are a combination of rainbows and browns, with an occasional cutt mixed in. You won't catch many that are slender. Most will weigh well over a pound. A three-pound fish won't excite many other fishermen, but if you catch one and fail to get excited yourself, I'd be glad to carry your rod for you while you rest.

Fees for the spring creeks vary slightly from water to water, greatly from season to season. You've got to reserve early. During the center of the best fishing, that means a year in advance. But off-season rates, November through May, are cheaper, rod time is easier to get, and the fishing is still too good for guys like me. It's an experience every angler should enjoy.

DePuy's Spring Creek, Rt. 38, Box 2267, Livingston, MT 59047, phone 406/222-0221. Armstrong Spring Creek, P.O. Box 955, Livingston, MT 59047, phone 406/222-2979. Nelson's Spring Creek, Rt. 38 Box 2022, Livingston, MT 59047, phone 406/222-2159.

A spring creek rainbow holds in such shallow water that it is clearly visible. But these trout feed on heavy hatches, are highly selective, and can be damnably difficult. Ben O. Williams

9

The Blue Iceberg

Ever-present geese fly over the tops of ice-rimed trees alongside the river. Dave Hughes

---

Facing page: Sidestream enters the main river in a cascade of ice during an arctic storm on the lower river above Billings. Dave Hughes

John Bailey kept telling me, "You've got to see the lower river. It's more than half of it. It's a wildlife sanctuary down there." He convinced me easily. The Yellowstone is the only major U.S. river that's left totally undammed, stem to stern, more than six hundred miles of it. When we think about trout, we think about the upper half: above the lake, Buffalo Ford, the Canyons, Paradise Valley. But the lower half of the river has its own surprises.

I kept putting off the trip to the lower river, playing catch-up on other parts of the Yellowstone, not getting to see everything I wanted to see even there. I scheduled a five-day float with Tony Robnett for September, but the same storm that sent Masako and me fleeing up Paradise Valley to Chico Hot Springs also muddied the Lamar, and sent silt sailing down the entire river. The lower river was unfishable. Tony and I wound up inside the Park, upstream from the Lamar, fishing, taking pictures of deer, elk, antelope, everything.

In fall, when most of the leaves are down, big browns move up to spawn, and can often be taken by casting streamers long across the broad, shallow tailouts of pools. Dale Spartas

It got to be October, and October was almost gone, before I launched my blue drift boat at Livingston in a snowstorm that was predicted to pass quickly. It didn't, and that started the brief but chilling story of the Blue Iceberg.

The air was a little below freezing when I launched. Snow swirled all around the boat and dimmed out the river downstream. That was balmy, about as good as conditions were going to get on the trip. But midges began hatching that first afternoon, and fish rose right between flakes of snow to take them. I rigged a rod, tied on a small Adams dry, and went after the trout. They were far from easy; trout are never easy when they nip at midges. But I hooked a few on a long flat. Then I got into an eddy that was nearly black with midges struggling to launch their little lives into that cold air. Not many made it.

Trout swirled in the eddy like sharks, feeding greedily, staying so near the top that their dorsal fins cut the surface as they cruised. I crouched down close to the eddy, just watched awhile, fascinated by the fierce predaceousness of these fish. They were propelled into the midst of the midges by the same instinct that caused *Tyrannosaurus rex* to crouch and ambush lumbering duck-billed dinosaurs near the same ground, so many asteroid impacts ago. Perhaps the same instinct, greatly attenuated, caused me to crouch and spy on the trout and prepare to ambush them.

I flicked a fly onto the surface. One of those dorsals cut toward it and in seconds a rainbow bounced up and did its aerial dance. It got off. I brought the fly in, redressed it with floatant, cast again, hooked another. I landed that one and let it go. A couple more takes put all the fish down in the eddy, so I pushed the boat out into the current and drifted down with the snow

again. A mink, startled at my approach, dashed loopingly through the riffling shelf of water that is the entrance of the Shields River and disappeared under the water.

Camp was on a cottonwood island, and I made a mistake by spreading the tarp under the tent rather than over the boat. The snow let up during the night, but everything in the boat was still buried by about four inches of white in the morning. I spent an hour bailing snow out of the boat, a new experience for a person who has bailed tons of water out of boats.

That second day the storm was predicted to expend itself. Instead an Arctic front blew in and rekindled it. Wind came up and got fierce, first flinging me downstream, then turning to needle snow into my cheeks and eyelids. Flocks of mallards and Canadian geese huddled on every riffle corner and sprang into the air with regret when the boat got too near. Halfway through the day I struggled into neoprene waders, not to go wading, rather to keep the lower half of my body warm. But I could not wear my wading shoes; they were frozen like bricks. So I set up camp that night walking over the soft thickness of snow in stocking foot waders, as if in slippers.

It's easy to gather cottonwood limbs on the islands. I heaped up a pile of them and lit a bonfire. After dark I pumped up the lantern, hung it in a tree, spread a garbage bag on the snow between the fire and the lantern and sat and read Conrad's *Lord Jim*, a book set in the tropics. Red sparks flew up from the fire; cold silver sparks that were specks of snow twirled down through the lantern light. It was beautiful: a frigid kind of beauty.

Fishing ended when the Arctic storm struck. The midge hatch seized up; no trout rose. It wouldn't have made any difference. The two rods I had rigged, one with a nymph and the other for dries, had icicles an inch long dangling from each guide. I could not have cast if I wanted to, which I didn't.

I covered the boat with the tarp that night and flung it off the next morning with a few more inches of snow on top. I launched into the wind, tried to eat breakfast of cereal in the boat, but milk kept liquid in the cooler froze a few minutes after I poured it into a bowl. My breakfast seized up like the midges. My hands hurt terribly. I warmed one and then the other inside my waders, holding both oars with one hand. But the wind cut instantly through my insulated ski gloves. Finally I let the oars trail in the water and warmed both hands at once. It was a mistake.

The wind gusted around and gave the boat a shove from behind. The downstream oar dug into the water, dipped under the boat, nearly flipped it, and almost broke before popping out of the oarlock. It floated a couple of feet from the boat until I scrabbled after it and got my hands wet fetching it. I shipped the oars, warmed both hands for awhile inside my waders and put on dry gloves that were not insulated. Things began to get dangerous.

The boat carried about two hundred pounds of ice and snow. Its sides were sheathed. The oars accumulated ice and got so heavy I had to chip it away every hour. All of my drinking water was frozen by then, and all the food inside the cooler froze as hard as stones.

♦

Nothing is more beautiful than a Yellowstone brown trout that is caught in the fall of the year along the lower river. Sue Wynkoop

I noticed some sort of whitish scum in the water, but paid little attention to it, though the back of my mind sent the nagging message to the front of my mind that this was the beginnings of ice. I ignored it. A herd of deer browsed on a willow island. I chose it as camp, assuming if the deer hung out there it must be a warm spot. The deer dropped down to the end of the island and splashed across to the mainland as if it was summer, not winter.

This was a five-day, one hundred mile trip. I had shuttled my pickup and trailer by Greyhound bus before launching. The rig waited at Laurel, near Billings, which is why I kept plodding on when I should have tied up the boat, hiked cross country to the freeway, and gotten out of there until things thawed out, returning to retrieve the boat later. But once I set a goal I like to get there, and usually keep going even when I know I shouldn't. I kept on, passing boat ramps at Big Timber and Columbus.

The next day that hint of slush ice could no longer be ignored. It gathered up in the long pools, bobbed along with the boat, then got scattered by the rapids. It was white on top, an inch out of water and four or five inches deep under the water. I played with it, slicing the soft bergs in half with my oars. The sun came out, shined on things but failed to warm them. Still, the sun was a cheerful sight, and it kept me going down the river.

But by late afternoon the sprinkled rafts of floating ice began to link up and join into sheets, still flowing with the river but now covering it in the pools, with open floes that I could slide into and maneuver along. But at times I got surrounded, got locked in, could not control the boat until the moment the river broke over into a rapid and the ice got broken up by it. By the end of the day I could no longer choose my route into a rapid, but could still maneuver once inside it. Coming out of each rapid the ice choked up in the pools. It still moved along at the speed of the river, but entirely covered it. The ice was now about a foot deep, still slushy, but too much mass to move with oars. I simply could not make the boat move once it got jammed up.

♦

When conditions get right, during the long Indian summer of a Montana fall, fishing the lower Yellowstone River can let you lead some trophy trout into your hand. Dale Spartas

Floe ice butts against the yellow sandstone bluffs on the lower Yellowstone. These are part of the formations that gave the river its name. Dave Hughes

The author awoke each morning on his trip to a tent that was covered with snow. Dave Hughes

I noticed a couple of things. First, I became more prone to mistakes as things got worse. Second, the river and the weather presented many more opportunities to make mistakes. When it finally seeped into me that a mistake would be fatal, I snapped myself awake and forced a combination of vigilance and caution. I knew that if I got into that water I would die. The air temperature fell far below the lowest mark on my stream thermometer. Later I learned it was around twenty below zero, the wind chill a lot lower than that.

The final day the river was rimmed with sheet ice. I had to break the boat out with my axe, and knocked a few hundred pounds of ice off the boat while I was at it. I launched and the floe ice, still nearly solid but still sliding downstream, drove me along the bank for a hundred yards before I could force the boat far enough out to escape sweepers, which arose at random and hissed at me with a sinister voice. The entire river began to hiss. I couldn't figure it out. Then I noticed the interface where flowing ice swept along ice anchored to the shore, grating against it, hissing.

There was truly a beauty in this trip that I'll never witness again, because I'll never do such a thing again. In case you haven't picked it up yet, I'm delicately dropping the hint that you shouldn't do this either. If the river starts to freeze up, get off, even if you have to leave your boat behind.

The beauty was brittle. Cottonwood trees were frozen masses of white. The sun struck down through them, igniting everything. Mist rose off the river, made everything mysterious, also made it impossible to read the river, to see where the boat, locked in ice anyway, was going to take me. Ducks and geese, frozen out elsewhere, gathered by the thousands on the river. I saw no hunters, and wondered why until I read about the temperatures later, and learned that two elk hunters froze to death in the same storm.

The geese were wary, but because of conditions they would have been easy to shoot. They watched the boat approach, let it get near, reluctant to fly. They probably thought it was just another ice berg drifting down the river. I now call the boat "The Blue Iceberg."

My constant fear, as I approached the takeout at Laurel, was getting locked into the ice and swept on past town. I didn't know where I'd wind up if that happened: Billings, Glendive, St. Louis? So I kept tight to the right shore and worried. My fears nearly came true.

The approach to town looked easy at first: the river swept out toward a bridge abutment, then back in toward the ramp. All I'd have to do was ride the right bank right to the ramp. But as I drew down closer to the bridge I noticed that the right bank turned into an ice peninsula probing far out toward the bridge piling.

The river dipped under this ice, and I had to go around the point or risk dipping under the ice with it, which didn't seem like a pleasant idea. So I rowed out a few feet and got caught in floe ice which came within two inches of bashing the boat into the bridge. Then I found myself separated from shore by a twenty foot strip of solid ice. I tried frantically to row through it, but could not split or budge it and saw the ramp and saw myself being swept downstream just fifty feet out from shore. I envisioned myself being swept on down the river forever.

I stopped rowing, looked around desperately, spotted a lead opening up just above me. I rowed upstream into it, forced the boat through it, strained my back getting the boat to the bank right at the ramp.

It took two hours to sweep eight inches of snow off the pickup, carry all my gear up the ramp, winch the boat all the way up because I couldn't back down the snowbound ramp without risking leaving my rig right there for the winter. I took a motel in town, had a hot bath, a soak in the hot tub, a hot shower. Then I ate a hot meal, went back to my room, had another hot bath, hot tub, and hot shower.

That's as far as I got down the river. It's the most beautiful part of it, though not in the most pristine way. Its fishing was great, what little I got of it that first midge afternoon. I'd love to do it again.

But next time in better weather.

♦

The Blue Iceberg at rest, covered with ice and snow, in a foggy dawn on the lower Yellowstone River during an arctic storm that caught the author on the river. Dave Hughes

10

Bighorn

The broad Bighorn offers plenty of places where you can park a boat, get out and wade to fish over pods of trout rising selectively to insect hatches. Dave Hughes

◆

Facing page: The Bighorn River has perhaps the most condensed population of trophy sized brown trout of any river in the world. It is the place to go when you want some assurance of holding one in your hands. Dave Hughes

The Bighorn River is a rare one, heading in Wyoming as the Wind River, already a large river when it enters Wind River Canyon, already famous for its trophy fishing, then emerging from the canyon with a new name: Bighorn. Under its new title it enters and exits Yellowtail Dam, flows across the plains of south-central Montana, and joins the Yellowstone River downstream from Billings.

Before closing of the dam in 1968, the lower Bighorn was a warmwater fishery. It was silty, and didn't hold many trout. But the dam served as a settling basin. It's depth cooled the water that emerged. Insects and other food forms that feed trout sprang into magnificent populations. Introduced trout, rainbows from the West and browns from the East, thrived and expanded in both numbers and size.

Today the Bighorn is perhaps the most likely place in the world to trick a trophy trout. It's a bad day on the river when you don't feel the tug of a two-pounder. There's nothing rare

This plump rainbow was hooked up at the riffle corner behind the angler, but its fight ended far downstream. Jim Schollmeyer

about holding a three- to four-pounder wet and dripping in your hands. It contains lots of trout even larger than that.

Bighorn River trout can be foolish. I once anchored my boat off to the side of a current tongue where it sliced into a giant pool, two hundred yards long. All the trout from the length of this pool had apparently gathered up at the head of it, anxious for the feed delivered down on the current from above. Little Olive mayflies hatched upstream. I'd been up there surprising a few fish with a size 16 dry. But I tied on an olive wet fly in the same size to fish across the current tongue.

I cast the wet out and let it swing down and around. Just as it left the current and entered the eddy off to the side, I felt a thump. It was not necessary to set the hook; the trout did that for me. I played the fish, netted it alongside the boat, admired its gold flanks and big black spots. It was a brown, sixteen inches long, around two pounds. I released it, cast again, hooked another.

When I finally upped the anchor a long time later, it was not because the fish had quit, but because I had to get to shore and tend to the watering of some cactus. I'd been standing in the boat

for hours, casting and catching fish. They averaged the same as the first, but some of them pushed up toward twenty inches, and were plenty hefty when held in the hands.

Bighorn River trout can be big. I once watched from across the river while Jim Schollmeyer fished his way up a riffle that was four feet deep, rumpled on top, dimpled by occasional feeding fish. Caddis flitted in the air, so Jim paused to tie on his own creation, the Deer Hair Caddis, in the same size as the naturals, a size 14. Then he covered the water in standard dry fly procedure, just like you'd fish a riffle on your own home stream, with upstream casts and downstream dead-drift floats. That's all. He stung several fish, brought half a dozen of them flopping into his hands.

Then he made a cast not unlike any of the others. A trout came up, Jim raised the rod and set the hook into it, his leader tippet broke against weight. A rainbow bounced angrily into the air above the riffle, the fly still pinned in its lip. It's outline from my distant view was long, plump. Jim's hands came together and his shoulders sagged, the posture of somebody who has lost a fish he wished he had caught. A burst of words tumbled across the river to me. I missed them but not their meaning. I called, "What did you say?"

Bighorn flats are smooth, and the trout fussy about what you try to feed them. It takes some careful casting to get a fish up and dancing. Dave Hughes

◆

"It must have weighed five pounds," Jim hollered, which is not what I think he said the first time.

Bighorn River trout can be picky. Rick Hafele is co-author of *Western Hatches.* He knows insects and the flies that match them. He is expert at the tactics for presenting those flies exactly the way trout want to see them. We fished a Bighorn flat together a few years back, over a heavy hatch of tiny *Baetis* duns. I couldn't get a single fish to nip at my flies. Rick had a hard time, too. But he changed flies and suddenly got into them, fishing the same water, using the same casts, doing everything I was doing but doing it with distressingly different results.

I splashed right over to him and asked, "What you using?"

"A Harrop Hairwing Dun," he said. At that time, I'd never heard of such a thing. Since that day I've caught many trout on such things.

"Let's see it," I said. It looked more like an Elk Hair Caddis than any mayfly imitation I'd ever seen. It's wings were deer hair tilted back, not fragile feather leaning forward like the wings on most mayfly dressings. If you think about it a bit, that's the way natural mayfly wings tilt, too: back over their bodies. Rick read about the fly in a magazine article just before we left for the Bighorn. He tied half a dozen, which isn't many for a one-week trip.

I stood at his shoulder and whined until he gave me one of his precious flies. I splashed off happy and caught some fish of my own, using the very same tactics I'd used before with all of my standard olive imitations.

Bighorn hatches can be heavy. When they are you've got to be able to match them or be frustrated. Of course, you can always fish nymphs.

The riverbed is alarmingly rich. Because flows are stabilized by the dam, vegetation gets a chance to take root. It is an aquatic pasture, browsed by an infinity of aquatic insects and crustaceans. Populations of mayfly nymphs and caddisfly larvae clamber through the weeds, are almost overwhelming, though of course

it's difficult to overwhelm a herd of hungry trout. Clumsy scuds scurry about and get intercepted on their errands. Oligochetes—worms that burrow into the bottom gravels—show up in kick net samples, hemoglobin turning some of them bright red. That is why the San Juan Worm, in all of its simplicity and indignity, is one of the best nymphs to use on the river.

But standard nymphs will work, too, if you just remember to use them small enough. Folks who haven't fished the river tend to use big nymphs because the river holds so many big trout. After all, they reason, big fish must hunger after bigger bites. It's not true. The average insect they eat, day after day, is about a size 16. Keep your nymphs to that same size and you'll find yourself entertaining lots more fish.

Hare's Ears, Zug Bugs, Pheasant Tails, Squirrel Nymphs: all work well. So will your favorites. If you don't own favorites check with the fly shops in Fort Smith and St. Xavior. They will be in close touch with what is working at the moment.

The best nymph tactic is the split shot and strike indicator method. Use enough shot to get the chosen fly to the bottom. Place the indicator up the leader about twice the depth of the water. Make your casts upstream, or up and across, and mend line often enough to keep the indicator floating freely, dangling the fly temptingly along the bottom.

Dry flies should most often match hatches. That doesn't mean you've always got to get complicated. One of the heaviest hatches on the river is a Hydropsychid caddis that's matched

◆

One of the best ways to see the Bighorn is to pop a small drift boat into the river, paddle idly downstream, stop once in a while to get a bend in your rod. Dave Hughes

almost perfectly with the standard Elk Hair in size 14 or 16. It comes off in September, toward evening. The first time my friends and I fished the river, we learned that you must retreat into stocking caps and hooded jackets to keep the caddis from

Bighorn trout spend most ot their time feeding on small insect hatches, such as this size 16 Little Olive Dun (Beatis). Dave Hughes

Preceding page: A pram or drift boat affords excellent transportation down the Bighorn and gets you into water where you'll have the nymphing drifts all to yourself. Dave Hughes

crawling down the back of your neck and even into your ears. They're that thick.

An earlier caddis, a Brachycentrid, is tiny and almost black. You can match it with a size 16 or 18 Deer Hair Caddis. But most often I use a soft-hackled wet fly, either a Starling and Black or Starling and Herl, in size 16 or 18.

The heaviest mayfly hatches are Little Olives and Pale Morning Duns *(Ephemerella)*. Match the first with Comparaduns or Hairwing Duns in size 18 and 20. The latter are the equivalent in color to Eastern sulfurs, though they belong to a different genus. Match them with pale yellow-olive Comparaduns or Hairwing Duns in size 16 and 18. But it's always best to check with the fly shops for the favorite fly of the moment. I would never visit the river myself without doing that, though I often arrive with bulging fly boxes. On a river with such a diversity of life, you never know precisely what will be hatching when you get there.

You don't really need to match hatches or fish nymphs in order to catch trout on the Bighorn. One of the best tactics is to float along in a boat, forty or fifty feet from the bank, hitting every indent and feature with a streamer. An olive or black Woolly Bugger, in size 6 or 8, works best for me, but your favorite will work best for you because you've got confidence in it. Some of the trout you'll stun this way are larger than the average fish you'll take when matching hatches.

The Bighorn is a big river, and it's truly best to appreciate it by boat. It has thirteen miles of fishable water below Yellowtail Dam, with three launch sites. There are no rapids, though there is one section with some bounce to it. But you can go around the

Working the water alongside the banks can often get you into Bighorn trout that others overlook. Jim Schollmeyer

back side of an island to avoid even that minor rumple; check with the fly shops, they'll give you a map of the river. They'll also rent you a boat, and even do the shuttle for you. But you'd best call far in advance to arrange it.

You can hike up and down river from any of the access sites, and in truth fish plenty of water, encounter plenty of rising trout. The best part of the Bighorn flows through the Crow Indian Reservation. Be sure to respect their property rights by staying within the high water mark of the river.

◆

A typical Bighorn River brown caught sipping insects in a backwater gets tipped back into the water to rest and get ready to fight again. Jim Schollmeyer

The Bighorn is not without problems. In low water years, when discharge from the dam is reduced, it can become choked with weeds, difficult to fish. Hatches get unsettled, and it's hard to figure out what's happening. The trout are still there, but it's more difficult to catch them, or to enjoy fishing for them. But in normal years the river is wide, clean, green on the bottom, handsome to the eye. That is, it's a handsome river in its upper thirteen miles.

The next twenty miles of river carries the same potential, but is knocked out most of the summer season by returning irrigation flows. It's dirty, a sort of grayish color that silts the bottom, reduces hatches, reduces vision of the trout. Because insect and crustacean populations are not so heavy, the number of fish is down. If returning irrigation water could be settled out before being dumped back into the river, it would more than double the fishing opportunities on this river that is already wonderful.

Another problem is crowding. There's no avoiding other folks when you fish the Bighorn. If you're after a pristine experience, simply don't go there. You won't find it. You'll find crowds at the boat ramps, other anglers working most of the water. If you care to be combative, you'll have no trouble finding somebody else of like nature to cooperate with you. But it's also easy to wander off a ways, find a pod of trout of your own, and

work over them largely undisturbed by the intrusion of other anglers. Most of them will leave you alone and go look for their own pod of rising trout.

Some of them don't know the etiquette of rivers, and will wade into your water, or cross your pod in a boat. I had this happen to me once. Three gentlemen in a boat drifted nearly under my rod tip and scattered the trout I had stalked so carefully. One of them asked, "How's fishing?"

I didn't want to start a quarrel. But this was close to the ramp. They had just launched and were headed down the whole crowded river. For their sake, and that of others, I didn't want them to keep on thinking it was all right to drive over other peoples' pods. So I said, "Fishing was fine until you rowed over my fish."

They did not accept this quietly or kindly. They were still shouting at me as they drifted out of sight around a far corner. The last thing I heard was, "If you'd learn how to fish, guys like us wouldn't bother you." The truth is, even if I did know how to fish as well as I wished, guys like that would still bother me. But I suspect the three of them took wide turns around the rest of the fishermen they encountered that day, which is all that I wanted to happen.

You take wide turns around other fishermen, too, and I'll do the same for you.

◆

The Bighorn is a placid tailwater flowing through a flat valley, its flow stabilized by Yellowtail Dam. The reservoir cools the water, grows plankton that enriches the downstream releases, causes the river to be excellent habitat for trout. Dave Hughes

John Bailey's favorite streamers and nymphs for the Yellowstone River: (top row, left to right) Bitch Creek Nymph, Rubber Leg Brown Stone, Gold Ribbed Hare's Ear, Caddis Pupa; (middle row) Spuddler, Kiwi Muddler, Dark Spruce, Light Spruce; (bottom row) Black Girdle Bugger, Black Krystal Bugger, Brown Woolly Worm, Muddler. Photo by Jim Schollmeyer

John Bailey is the second-generation owner of Dan Bailey's Fly Shop in Livingston, Montana. His father left the East in the 1930s, started his fly shop in the center of the world's best trout fishing, became a legend on the Yellowstone River. He was known both for his knowledge as a fisherman and his willingness to fight conservation battles for the river whenever a threat to it arose, which over the years was often. John was raised fishing the Yellowstone River. Today he runs Dan Bailey's and has taken up the conservation battles his father fought.

George Anderson is owner of George Anderson's Yellowstone Angler Fly Shop in Livingston, Montana. He is well-known for his writings about fly fishing, primarily articles about nymphing the Yellowstone River and its spring creek tributaries. He is originator of the Rubber Leg Brown Stone, Olive and Cream Peeking Caddis, and George's Brown Stone Nymph. In 1989 he set the Jackson Hole One-Fly record by taking 78 cutthroat trout on one Rubber Leg Brown Stone.

◆

George Anderson's favorite nymphs for the Yellowstone River and its tributaries: (top row, left to right) Prince Nymph, Flash Back Hare's Ear, Olive Peeking Caddis, Cream Peeking Caddis, Netbuilding Caddis, (middle row) Bitch Creek Nymph, Red Squirrel Nymph, George's Brown Stone Nymph, Rubber Leg Brown Stone; (bottom row) Lead Eye Woolly Bugger, Brook's Stone, Yuk Bug, Ultra Yuk Bug. Photo by Jim Schollmeyer

Richard Park's favorite dry flies for the Yellowstone River (top row, left to right) Salmon Fly, Coachman Trude, Letort Hopper, Parachute Baetis; (middle row) Elk Caddis, Griffith's Gnat, Joe's Hopper, Royal Wulff; (bottom row) Hairwing Variant, Light Hendrickson, Quill Gordon, Adams. Photo by Jim Schollmeyer

◆

Richard Parks took over the helm of Park's Fly Shop, in Gardner, Montana where the Yellowstone River exits the park, after a tour of duty in Viet Nam in the 1970s. He now guides on the river almost daily throughout the long summer season. His expertise is the dry fly; he is co-author of the book *Tying and Fishing the West's Best Dry Flies.*

DALE SPARTAS

Tom Travis and his wife Krys are owners of Montana's Master Angler Fly Shop in Livingston, Montana. Throughout the summer season, Tom spends most of his days guiding, and manages to put many hours in on the Paradise Valley spring creeks, both fishing and guiding. He has done research over the years that has led to a series of informational sheets on the Yellowstone River, on waters in the Park, and on the spring creeks: what flies and methods to use during the various seasons.

Tom Travis's favorite Yellowstone-area spring creek flies: (top row, left to right) Tom's Brass Wire Midge Nymph, Tom's Pale Olive Midge Worm, Tom's Black Midge Pupa, Tom's Emerging Black & White Para Midge, Tom's Gray Shuck Trailing Midge Adult; (middle row) Tom's Multi-Purpose Midge Adult, Tom's New Dubb Gray Midge Adult, Sawyer Pheasant Tail Nymph, Tom's Olive Sawyer Nymph, Tom's Shuck Trailing Foam Nymph: Pale Morning Dun; (bottom row) Tom's shuck Trailing PMD Thorax Dun, Tom's K-Flash Trico Dun Parachute, Tom's Rusty Spinner, Tom's Male Trico Spinner. Photo by Jim Schollmeyer

Bibliography

Alt, David and Donald W. Hyndman: *Roadside Geology of Montana.* Missoula: Mountain Press Publishing Company, 1986.

Bakeless, John: *The Journals of Lewis and Clark.* New York: New American Library, 1964.

Colbert, Edwin H.: "Mammoths and Men". Natural History Magazine, 1940 (from Ternes, Alan, Ed.: *Ants, Indians, and Little Dinosaurs.* New York: Charles Scribner's Sons, 1975.)

Ekey, Robert: *Yellowstone On Fire!* Billings: Billings Gazette, 1989.

Fischer, Hank: *The Floater's Guide to Montana.* Missoula: Falcon Press, 1986.

Fritz, William J.: *Roadside Geology of the Yellowstone Country.* Missoula: Mountain Press Publishing Company, 1985.

Hafele, Rick and Dave Hughes: *Western Hatches.* Portland: Frank Amato Publications, 1981.

Haines, Aubrey: *The Yellowstone Story, Volumes One and Two.* Yellowstone National Park: Yellowstone Library and Museum Association, 1977

Hoxie, Frederick E.: *The Crow.* New York: Chelsea House Publishers, 1989.

Hughes, Dave: *American Fly Tying Manual.* Portland: Frank Amato Publications, 1986.

Western Streamside Guide. Portland: Frank Amato Publications, 1987.

Janetski, Joel C., *Indians of Yellowstone Park.* Salt Lake City: University of Utah Press, 1987.

Jones, Jayne Clark: *The American Indian in America, Volume I.* Minneapolis: Lerner Publications, 1973.

The American Indian in America, Volume II. Minneapolis: Lerner Publications, 1973.

Krakell, Dean, II: *Downriver: A Yellowstone Journey.* San Francisco: Sierra Club Books, 1987.

Martin, Paul S.: "Pleistocene Overkill". Natural History Magazine, 1967 (from Ternes, Alan, Ed.: *Ants, Indians, and Little Dinosaurs.* New York: Charles Scribner's Sons, 1975.)

Mathews, Craig and John Juracek: *Fly Patterns Of Yellowtone.* West Yellowstone: Blue Ribbon Flies, 1987.

Parsons, Willard H.: *Middle Rockies and Yellowstone.* Dubuque: Kendall/Hunt Publishing Copmpany, 1978.

Russell, Dale A.: *An Odyssey In Time: The Dynosaurs of North America.* New York: North Word Press/National Museum of Natural Sciences, 1989.

Russell, Osborne: *Journal of a Trapper.* Lincoln: University of Nebraska Press, 1965.

Schneider, Bill: *Montana's Yellowstone River.* Helena: Montana Magazine, 1985.

Varley, John D. and Paul Schullery: *Freshwater Wilderness: Yellowstone Fishes & Their World.* Yellowstone National Park: Yellowstone Library and Museum Association, 1983.

Shish kebabs taste better because you're "out there," far into the backcountry, cooking them over an open flame. Masako Tani